TUDOR ECONOMIC PROBLEMS

THE MEN AND IDEAS SERIES

General Editor: R. W. Harris

Master of Studies and Head of the History Department
The King's School, Canterbury

THE FIRST THREE VOLUMES:

I TUDOR ECONOMIC PROBLEMS
by Peter Ramsey

Lecturer in History, the University of Bristol

II POLITICAL IDEAS 1760–1792
by R. W. Harris

III THE LIBERAL PARTY FROM
EARL GREY TO ASQUITH
by R. B. McCallum

Master of Pembroke, Oxford

THE MEN AND IDEAS SERIES

I

TUDOR ECONOMIC PROBLEMS

by

PETER RAMSEY

LONDON

VICTOR GOLLANCZ LTD

1972

First Published March 1963
Second Impression January 1965
Third Impression October 1966
Fourth Impression October 1968
Fifth Impression June 1972

ISBN 0 575 00253 0

PRINTED IN GREAT BRITAIN
BY EBENEZER BAYLIS AND SON, LTD.
THE TRINITY PRESS, WORCESTER, AND LONDON

ACKNOWLEDGMENT

In a general work of this nature the author's debts are so numerous and diffuse that no adequate acknowledgment of them is possible. My own borrowings from the printed works on Tudor economic history will be apparent on every page. More particularly I should like to thank Dr. L. A. Parker and Miss Helen Miller for permission to make use of material in their unpublished theses. I also gratefully acknowledge the early guidance of Dr. G. D. Ramsay, who first introduced me to the problems of 16th century trade. More recently I have become deeply indebted to my colleague, Mr. P. V. McGrath, who read the whole of this book in typescript and made many helpful suggestions. The faults that have survived his careful scrutiny are due to my own wilful persistence in error.

CONTENTS

INTRODUCTION

WE HAVE NO DETAILED contemporary description of England when the Tudors first began to rule. The *Relation of the Island of England*, written by an anonymous Venetian about the year 1500, is the nearest approach to one. It abounds in shrewd and sometimes surprising comments on the English character, some of which may or may not apply today:

> The English are great lovers of themselves, and of everything belonging to them; they think that there are no other men than themselves, and no other world but England; and whenever they see a handsome foreigner, they say that "he looks like an Englishman," and that "it is a great pity that he should not be an Englishman,"

— or —

> They have an antipathy to foreigners, and imagine that they never come into their island, but to make themselves masters of it, and to usurp their goods; neither have they any sincere and solid friendships amongst themselves, . . . And although their dispositions are somewhat licentious, I never have noticed anyone, either at court or amongst the lower orders, to be in love; whence one must necessarily conclude, either that the English are the most discreet lovers in the world, or that they are incapable of love; I say this of the men, for I understand it is quite the contrary with the women, who are very violent in their passions. Howbeit the English keep a very jealous guard over their wives, though anything may be compensated in the end, by the power of money.

The avarice of Englishmen was noted by others, it may be said. It was remarked that they were so bent on their profits in the Netherlands trade that "if Englishmen's fathers were hanged in Antwerp's gate, their children would creep betwixt their legs to come into the said town." But such observations, even when confirmed, do not help us very much to understand the economic and social structure of early Tudor England, and when he comes to describe the towns and the countryside, and the occupations of its inhabitants, our Italian visitor proves disappointing. He enthuses over the wealth and magnificence of London—especially the goldsmiths of the Strand—but finds space for only a passing reference to York and Bristol, and thinks no other city worth a mention. He remarks on the low density of population, inevitably striking to an Italian, and on the wealth of the soil (which he thinks inadequately exploited). He refers also to the great production of lead and tin, of which his own country was a principal importer. But the woollen textile industry seems to have escaped his notice, and the sum total of his remarks on economic matters is meagre in the extreme. It is not from his graceful pages that we can reconstruct the England of 1500.

More comprehensive and useful is the *Itinerary* of the antiquary John Leland, compiled after his death from the rough jottings that he made during his extensive travels in the years 1535–43. Even in their edited form these notes are far from being a comprehensive description of the realm, and certainly they lack the literary grace of the Italian *Relation*. But Leland was a conscientious and literal-minded observer, who deserves the title of "father of English topography", and the very lack of form has advantages for the modern historian; much valuable detail might have been lost if the traveller had retained his reason and life long enough to edit and select. Since, too, the pace of economic change was so much slower in the 16th century than in our own day, the England of Leland's travels was not so very different from that of 1485. But it was very different from that of the 20th century.

England was still overwhelmingly an agrarian community. The great mass of her population lived by and on the land, and the typical unit was the village, not the city. There was indeed only one city, judging by modern standards, and London's population (perhaps 80,000 in 1545) was quite exceptional. Other cities, such as Norwich (about 17,000),

Bristol (10,000) or Exeter (8000) would be to our eyes no
more than small country towns. And the towns that Leland
lists so indefatigably seem to us often no more than villages;
some had but a single street, and the possession of four streets
called for special remark. The countryside extended right
into such towns, and their inhabitants should be thought of
as countrymen and not as towndwellers. Farming, whether
arable or pastoral, was the national occupation, and though
many husbandmen might combine domestic industry with
tillage only a minority of the population lived by trade or industry alone. Early 16th century England was not remotely
a nation of shopkeepers or the workshop of the world.

The face of the countryside itself has changed a good deal
since Leland. Gone are most of the private parks that he
describes, and which the Italian visitor exuberantly estimated at four thousand. Every substantial landowner still
had his park—sometimes two—where deer were carefully
preserved. The loss to agriculture must have been quite considerable, both through destruction of crops and the sheer
acreage withdrawn from cultivation. Sometimes these parks
are described as "forests", which implies a more imposing
extent than they really possessed, but there were still great
areas—the forests of Sherwood, Epping and Arden, to mention but three—which had resisted the depredations of
growing sheep flocks. By this date they were fast diminishing, and housed a dwindling number of wild fauna. The demands of industry—housing, shipbuilding and ironworks—
were fast eating away the country's natural wealth of timber, and well before the end of the century its preservation
had become a serious problem. The emphasis had, however,
changed; by 1600 forests were maintained as a source of
naval supplies, not as before for the pleasures of the chase.

There were also large areas of fen and marshland that
still awaited drainage and reclamation. The East Anglian
fens continued to wait until the early 17th century. In Lincolnshire the Commissioners of Sewers fought an unending
battle with the waters, and generally speaking held their own

even if they did little to reclaim new territory. But the county was so isolated by rivers that it has been described as "virtually a peninsula" in the 16th century, and contemporaries regarded it as remote and almost uninhabitable. In 1592 a prisoner wrote to the Lord Admiral:

> If I am grievous in your honour's hearing or sight, let me be banished in the Brill, Flushing, Lincolnshire or in the worst place of her Majesty's dominions, or to some vile war without pay, so I am not left in this cage of misery.

Lincolnshire, it would seem, was only one degree better than prison.

Though enclosure of the open fields had begun long before 1485, and was already well-established in Kent and the west country, great stretches of champaign country still survived into the 16th century, and most of them would continue to survive until the 18th century. Few of them were rich enough to bear wheat-crops, and barley, oats, rye and beans were their staple products. Intensive marling sometimes made good the natural deficiencies of the soil, and Leland noted its use on the sandy soils of Shropshire, Cheshire and Lancashire. But a general absence of manures made a high level of production unlikely, and difficulties of transport did not encourage farmers to seek it. London and a few other towns provided more than a strictly local market, but for many areas subsistence farming was the rule and no more was produced than could be consumed locally.

Communications were far from easy in Tudor England, though the country was no worse equipped with roads than France or Germany. Broadly speaking, the roads were adequate for light transport where they ran over the chalklands or lighter soils, but were liable to become impassable where they crossed belts of clay. Local enterprise and benefactions did something to maintain both roads and bridges, but there is little doubt that travel was more difficult in the 16th century than in Roman Britain—at least as between London and other main centres. Bulk transport by road was difficult, and building materials were carried not more than ten or twelve miles; hence the regional differentiation of Tudor architecture, confined largely to the use of local materials. Fortunately transport was relatively easy in the wool-growing areas, while in the clay belts rivers could sometimes be used instead of roads. But rivers tended to be obstructed with weirs and bridges, and only a few main waterways—such as the Thames, Severn, Ouse and Trent—were easily navigable for long stretches. Small vessels could travel up the Severn as far as Shrewsbury, and the Trent was free from obstruction below Nottingham except for the bridge at Newark; on the other hand the upper Derwent was cluttered with bridges every three miles above Sutton, while sea-going vessels could go no further up the Exe than Topsham. In winter, when road surfaces deteriorated sharply, transport became acutely difficult and travel was best avoided.

Partly because of these difficulties Tudor England was much more varied and differentiated than it is today. The range of economic and social interchange was more restricted, and provincial loyalties and rivalries far more intense. It was at the county rather than the national level that the gentry competed for influence and prestige. Hence arose the lively struggles to secure nomination to the Commission of the Peace or to serve the county as knight of the shire in parliament. Lesser men looked to the local magnate for leadership and patronage, not to the court. To Cornishmen and Northumbrians London was a remote and alien place, and resentment towards an unpopular minister like Cromwell was often partly inspired by provincial jealousy of the capital. There was yet no common language, and local dialects were far more distinct. Cornish was still a living language in the south-west, and the new English prayer book of 1549 was said to be unintelligible there. It would be a long time before the use of printing and the cultural dominance of London produced a more or less standardised English, still more a standardised orthography. For another century and longer the erratic phonetic spelling of even the most literate people continued to reflect the wide diversity of the spoken word.

It would be a mistake, however, to regard Tudor society as immobile. Not only did men of all classes flock to London throughout the century; they also moved frequently and readily from one district to another. The tenurial records of the period and the Elizabethan muster rolls both show a high degree of mobility in rural society at its lower levels. It has been estimated that in 1641 only some 16 per cent of the agricultural population had lived a hundred years in the same village. Servants and artificers were a notoriously migrant class "which change and remove their dwellings daily". No doubt the rate of change was highest in the towns, where mortality rates were highest, but it is clear that the notion of a static, unchanging village is a myth. Farming methods may not have changed very much, but the farmers certainly did. Government legislation was intended not only to standardise industrial training and methods and provide an agrarian labour force; it was also trying to meet the problems caused by a highly mobile population that local institutions could not contain.

The range and intensity of this mobility is impossible to measure, and the over-all distribution of the population did not shift very much. It remained concentrated in the south, and travellers remarked how wealth and inhabitants diminished as one travelled north. It would be going too far to say that the Trent divided England into two nations, but there was an abiding antithesis between the south-east and the north-west counties. It was not only an antithesis of prosperity and population, but also of custom and tradition. New ideas spread from the south-east, and only slowly radiated outwards to more remote parts. It was entirely characteristic that in the 16th century Lancashire should be a stronghold of the old religion. It was not until the 19th century that it became a symbol of wealth and modernity.

In the late 15th and early 16th centuries the most significant fact about the population was not its mobility but its numerical increase. Unfortunately we are very ill-informed about this fundamental process, which may well be the most important development of the age. The whole medieval period affords only two reasonably reliable estimates of population—Domesday Book in 1086 and the Poll Tax returns of 1377—and there is no Tudor evidence that allows us to make a census at any one date. In his *British Medieval Population* J. C. Russell has made a careful estimate of trends from 1377 to 1545, but this is based on an assumed rate of growth from 1377 to 1690 and can be only partly confirmed by the evidence of chantry certificates. When other developments—such as enclosures and increases of prices and rents—are clearly linked with a rise in population, this absence of sound statistics is very regrettable. But for the moment we can only accept Russell's calculations as a provisional basis, and trust that further research will not show them to be too wide of the mark.

The broad outline of population movement in the later Middle Ages is as follows. The 13th century had seen a rapid growth, which was only slightly decelerating in the 1330's and 1340's. On the eve of the Black Death (1348) the population of England stood at about 3·75 million. A succession of plagues brought it down as low as 2·25 million by 1374, and by 1400 a further small decline had reduced it 2·1 million. From about 1430 there was increasingly rapid recovery, and for the year 1545 an estimate of 3·22 million seems reasonable. This is nearly 50 per cent above the figure for 1374, but still below the high-point of the mid-fourteenth century. Similar trends can be seen in France, where a very rapid recovery after 1460 may have brought the population up to 15 million by 1500, and in Italy, where a similar rise from about 1500 may have brought it to 8·85 million by 1550.

It can be seen at once that England was thinly populated by comparison with other western countries, and that her resources in manpower were particularly meagre if measured against those of France. The Italian visitor was not far wrong when he suggested that England could support a much larger population. But a rapid proportional increase still posed difficult problems of adaptation, and all the more so when contemporaries were but dimly aware of their basic cause. In a conservative and technically primitive society the process of adaptation was bound to be painful.

In some spheres there were clear gains. The general recovery of west European populations, especially those of the towns, meant healthier markets for traders and industrial producers, both at home and overseas. English cloth and wool merchants benefited from the widespread recovery in commerce that followed the relative stagnation of the early 15th century. The difficulties that they encountered in the mid-sixteenth century were not due to any general contraction of the European market, but to the collapse of the one particular market where they had concentrated all their efforts. This problem was obvious enough to make its solution reasonably practicable.

In agriculture the gains were not so clear, and the problems more acute. In the late 14th century the shrinkage of population had meant that land was relatively plentiful and food supplies normally quite adequate. Shortage of manpower enabled the peasantry to improve its financial and juridical position. A century later the situation was reversed. Land was becoming scarce again, and labour more plentiful. Pressure of population on food resources became more acute, especially since 15th century conditions had encouraged conversion of arable to pasture. To relieve the pressure it was necessary either to farm the existing arable more intensively or to reconvert pasture. Tudor farming technique was inadequate to raise productivity very much, though enclosure of the open fields made possible some increase in efficiency. Reconversion was not likely to be popular with landlords who were profiting from a boom in the woollen industry. Thus there arose intensified competition for land, and between arable and pastoral farming. In such conditions farmers without security of tenure were sure to suffer, and the weakest would go to the wall.

Increased demand for food was bound to raise its price, and the Tudor period was in fact one of sustained and sometimes breakneck inflation. A number of different factors contributed to this, and it cannot be conclusively demonstrated that food shortage was the chief one. But the rise was peculiarly sharp for both food and rent, and this explanation seems the most likely one. It goes without saying that a general price rise accelerated, if it did not fundamentally alter, the process of social change. The struggle for economic survival became more bitter, the gap between success and failure became wider. And because inflation followed a long period of price-stability its problems seemed to contemporaries more dire and insoluble.

Many of the problems are still obscure to us, and with some justice this period has been classed among the "dark ages" of English economic history. Such topics as enclosures, inflation, the "rise of the middle class", the expansion of trade, are all controversial, and the apparent certainties of the older text-books have been resolved into doubts. We are more conscious than we used to be of the shortage of statistical data, and of the detailed researches that are needed before confident generalisations can be made. It is not the purpose of this book to supply a new set of certainties in place of the old. It is hoped only to state the present "state of the question" in a number of disputed fields, and to make some suggestions as to how the England of John Leland was grappling with its difficulties.

I

AGRARIAN PROBLEMS

ONE PROBLEM DOMINATED the minds of Tudor landlords and peasants, and of a government concerned for peace and order in the countryside—the problem of enclosures. This bulks so large in the legislation, the propaganda and the legal business of the period that it is easy to get a false impression of its nature and importance. What exactly did contemporaries understand by the word? Why did the problem arise at this particular date? Had it indeed arisen for the first time at the accession of the Tudors, or are we suffering from an optical illusion; is it only the evidence of widespread complaints and government concern with the problems that are new, not the problem itself? Was the problem at its most acute in the mid-century, as the activities of Protector Somerset's government and the outbreaks of agrarian trouble in 1548–49 might lead us to suppose? Was the whole country affected, or only limited areas? Who were the enclosers, and who the victims of their alleged greed and ruthlessness? How did the former set about their business, and how far could the latter defend themselves? Why were successive governments perturbed, and how far did they take effective action? And, finally, was the whole problem as great and pressing as contemporary agitation suggests?

These are all difficult questions, and the answers are still vexed and controversial. But they do need to be asked, and some answers attempted. This is the more necessary as the picture given in some text-books is highly misleading. It is still too easy to get the impression that the enclosure-movement was a uniform process spread over the entire countryside of England, first becoming acute under the early Tudors and reaching a climax in 1549; that profiteering, rack-renting and evictions were commonplace, that vast areas of arable land were converted to pasture, and that the whole English peasantry trembled under the threat or actuality of ruthless commercial landlordism. Whatever the truth of the matter is, it is certainly not that. It is hoped that the following pages will do something to modify this over-simplified and too catastrophic version.

When Tudor writers speak of enclosure they mean both less and more than a twentieth-century reader might understand by that word. They made an often tacit distinction between "good" and "bad" enclosures, and it is usually only the latter that they have in mind. The "good" enclosure took place when a farmer fenced off his own land, whether arable or pasture, in order to protect his stock and crops and to pursue more scientific methods than was otherwise possible. If the procedure led to increased production, as it often did, he rightly earned the praises of the agricultural publicists.

> Experience should seem plainly to prove that enclosures should be profitable, and not hurtful to the common weal; for we see that countries where most enclosures be are most wealthy, as Essex, Kent, Devonshire and such.

Thus the Knight, in the *Discourse of the Common Weal*. But the all-important proviso was that such enclosure must be effected without prejudicing or invading the rights of others. As long as it was achieved by mutual agreement among neighbours, or even when it was done unilaterally but without threatening the livelihood of the encloser's fellows, no reasonable objection could be raised. But all too often, it was alleged, the encloser acted at the expense of his neighbours and disregarded their rights. Unable to obtain their amicable consent to an exchange of lands that would allow him to consolidate his holdings, he forced tenants out of their holdings by threats and financial pressure. He did not confine himself to fencing off lands that were his to enclose, but also annexed parts of the common pasture of the village. The villagers were thus denied vital rights of pasturage for their sheep and cattle, rights that had been established by custom and convention and were inadequately protected at law. Unemployment and depopulation might also result. Even when the encloser continued arable farming on his enclosed lands he might easily effect labour economies and find it convenient to dispense with unnecessary houses standing on his enclosed fields. This risk was enormously increased when he converted arable to pasture, since the raising of sheep needed less men than corn, and enclosure followed by conversion could thus mean acute local unemployment. Enclosures of this kind were clearly "bad" enclosures, whatever the profits to those carrying them out. Thus when they speak of enclosures (unqualified) contemporaries normally have this category in mind, and are thinking not of the simple act of fencing off a farmer's own property but also of the social evils that all too often accompanied this act—violent eviction, depopulation and unemployment, normally associated either with the enclosing of commons or the conversion of arable to pasture. The distinction is made by the Doctor, answering the Knight in the *Discourse*:

> I mean not all enclosures, nor yet all commons, but only of such enclosures as turneth commonly arable fields into pastures; and violent enclosures without recompense of them that have right to common therein.

It is repeated by John Hales in 1548, when he instructs jurors empanelled to inquire into recent enclosures how they are to interpret the word:

> But first, to declare unto you what is meant by this word *inclosures*. It is not taken where a man doth enclose and hedge in his own proper ground, where no man hath commons. For such inclosure is very beneficial to the commonwealth; it is a cause of great encrease of wood: but it is meant thereby, when any man hath taken away and enclosed any other mens' commons, or hath pulled down houses of husbandry, and converted the lands from tillage to pasture. This is the meaning of this word, and so we pray you to remember it.

Tudor writers thus tended to confine the word to its abused form. In another direction they and later writers tended to extend its meaning. Some of the evils associated with exclosure might occur when no fences were erected. The consolidation of holdings could sometimes lead to the destruction of homesteads and reduced employment without enclosure of the area affected. In this case it is more accurate to talk of "engrossment" rather than enclosure. Conversion of arable to pasture could take place without any new fences or hedges being erected. Overstocking of the common with the sheep of a wealthy landlord might be a prelude to enclosure or might be simply a temporary abuse. "Enclosure" thus covers a multitude of sins, and leads the modern reader into confusion. Here the term will be restricted to the actual fencing-in of land. It will be applied chiefly to the two most controversial categories in the 16th century—the enclosure of arable land for conversion to pasture, and the enclosure of commons—two categories that need to be distinguished from one another.

Why did enclosure become an especially live issue in the 16th century? Partly the answer lies in an increase of population, especially urban population. Unfortunately no reliable figures are available for this, and we may be in danger of inventing a plausible hypothesis simply to explain away enclosures, the price-rise, wide-spread vagrancy and unemployment, and other embarrassing phenomena of the Tudor scene. But there is little doubt of a great increase in the population of London at least, which had reached perhaps 200,000 by the end of the century (some writers have suggested even 300,000). This produced an urgent demand for food, and the capital was making growing demands on an ever-widening area. The main sources of supply were inevitably the home counties, with Kent especially prominent as a supplier of cereals. Cereals came also from East Anglia, and even from as far as Lincolnshire, though the longer-range coastal shipments were significant only in years of exceptional difficulty. The more industrialized areas of the west country, the textile districts of Yorkshire, and Tyneside produced a similar demand for food on a much smaller scale, while some old-established cities like Bristol and Lincoln, declining in population at the beginning of the century, were recovering before its end. Farmers thus had a growing incentive to produce for the market rather than for local subsistence. Some such incentive had, of course, always existed, and it would be absurd to picture the medieval agrarian economy at any date as one of pure subsistence farming. But even in the 16th century there were areas where it might fairly be said that subsistence farming was still the rule, and it took a greatly increased incentive to break down the habits of centuries and provide the initiative to overcome the perennial problems of inland transport. Such an incentive was now being supplied.

To meet this growing demand for food the Tudor farmers had either to increase the area of land under cultivation or the efficiency of their methods. The 16th century saw no very spectacular extension of the area of land under cultivation, and large-scale schemes of land-reclamation like the draining of the Fens had to wait until the Stuart period. The alternative was therefore an increase in efficiency, and there was little doubt, contemporaries agreed, that enclosed and consolidated farms were more productive than holdings worked under an open-field system. The farmer with an eye to the growing food-market of London and other cities would thus seek to engross and enclose so as to increase his production and his profits.

A rising demand for food was, however, only one possible incentive to enclosure. It could be effective only in areas whose soil readily lent itself to more intensive cultivation and which had adequate transport to take advantage of growing markets. Adequate transport in this period meant primarily water-transport, so only coastal counties or those with good river communications with London and other cities were likely to be affected. Even these, it seems, were not vitally affected until the last decades of the century, when London's needs became really acute. Until then another incentive worked more powerfully. The demands of the growing woollen textile industry made production of wool even more profitable than the production of cereals for many farmers, and this prompted them to enclose, not to grow more corn but to convert arable to pasture and to seize for themselves as much of the common pasture of their district as they could lay hands on.

Early Tudor critics of the enclosure movement were unanimous in attributing it to the higher profits of sheep-farming and the natural covetousness of landlords who pursued these profits. (Their definition of enclosure excluded, as we have seen, enclosure for improved arable farming.)

> Who will maintain husbandry which is the nurse of every county as long as sheep bring so great gain? Who will be at the cost to keep a dozen in his house to milk kine, make cheese, carry it to the market, when one poor soul may by keeping sheep get him a greater profit? Who will not be contented for to pull down houses of husbandry so that he may stuff his bags full of money?

The Doctor in the *Discourse* alleges that

> there is more lucre by grazing of ten acres to the occupier alone than is in tillage of twenty and the causes thereof be many. One is that grazing requires small charge and small labour which in tillage consumes much of the master's gain.

Fitzherbert, author of one of the most widely-read text-books on farming, claims that the gain in enclosing land for pasture as against enclosing it for arable farming was as one pound to one mark, i.e. that it was 50 per cent more profitable. There was general agreement, then, that the high price of wool and the low labour costs of sheep-farming proved an irresistible temptation to covetous Tudor landlords.

How far does other evidence bear out these assertions? The boom in cloth exports during the first half of the century would certainly lead us to expect an increased demand for wool, and consequently better prices for wool-growers. Growth of population would lead to an increase in home consumption too, though we have no figures to show this. Mr. P. J. Bowden has recently constructed an index to show the movement of wool prices from 1450–1699. This shows very marked variations from year to year, but it is clear that prices increased rapidly in the first half of the century, especially in the 1530's and 1540's, and had about doubled by the middle of the century. But there was little increase in the second half. Prices were static or even falling in the period 1570–90, and though there was a sharp increase again in the 1590's it was not nearly as great as the increase in food prices at the same time.[1] Very broadly speaking, then, it might still pay to convert arable to pasture up to about 1550, provided that economies in labour could be made. To that extent the earlier commentators are confirmed. But after 1570 it probably paid better to reconvert from pasture to arable, provided the increase in labour costs did not offset the greater profit in selling grain.

Figures derived from the investigations of the commission of inquiry set up by Wolsey in 1517 tell a similar story for the early 16th century. In five Midland counties the enhanced rental values of land enclosed since 1488 show that it was at least 40 per cent more profitable to convert to pasture than to leave the enclosed holdings as arable. It is not surprising that in four of these counties (Oxfordshire, Buckinghamshire, Northamptonshire and Warwickshire) some 80 per cent of the 32,000 acres of enclosed land was pasture. In Berkshire, on the other hand, where the rental value of enclosed arable was nearly 14 per cent higher than that of pasture, less than 40 per cent of the new enclosures were for pasture. The returns of this commission of inquiry are far from complete, and these figures are therefore not wholly dependable. But they tell us, after all, just what we would expect—that Tudor landlords knew their business and enclosed for the greatest possible profit. Many of their contemporaries thought that their social conscience should have restrained them.

[1] See pp. 115-16 for the price movements of other consumables.

The evidence on the motives of enclosing landlords suggests a likely answer to the question of when the movement was at its height. If enclosure was associated with the expansion of the cloth industry and a relatively high price for wool as compared with grain, then we should expect it to be most active at the beginning of our period. It was in the reign of Henry VII that cloth-exports rose most rapidly. Was enclosure most active then also?

The evidence of the 1517 commission suggests that it was. In both Warwickshire and Nottinghamshire it was found that most of the enclosing activity since 1488 had taken place before 1500, and this is all the more remarkable when we bear in mind that it was the more recent enclosures that witnesses before the commission were likely to remember. We are unfortunately very ill-informed about late-15th century enclosures, but the first statute aimed against them, that of 1489, implies that even then they were not a new problem. There is, moreover, the evidence of the Warwickshire historian John Rous, who at his death in 1491 left an unprinted manuscript of a history of the kings of England. In it he lists no fewer than 58 depopulated villages in his own county and adjoining ones, and laments that "if such destruction as that in Warwickshire took place in other parts of the country it would be a national danger." He himself had petitioned parliament in 1459. There is thus a considerable, if not conclusive, body of evidence to suggest that enclosures were at a peak at the accession of Henry Tudor, if not before, and that they may have been on the wane by 1517.

Detailed figures are available for enclosures in Leicestershire, one of the worst-hit counties. In the period 1485–1607 a total of 31,000 acres are known to have been enclosed. About 33 per cent of them were enclosed in the years 1485–1510, and only 19 per cent for the whole period 1511–1580. The decade 1541–50 was that least affected— less than half of one per cent of the enclosures of the century took place in those ten years. From 1580 onwards the movement was one of crescendo, accounting for 48 per cent of the whole with 27 per cent falling in the years 1601–07. In brief, the picture is one of two active periods of enclosing at the very beginning and end of the Tudor period, with a comparative lull in the middle decades. This is the reverse of what we might expect from the intensive propaganda of the mid-century, but quite consistent with the more strictly economic evidence.

The Inquisitions of Depopulation made after the Midland revolt of 1607 amplify the general picture. They cover some 70,000 acres enclosed in six Midland counties in 1578–1607. The same crescendo is apparent. Some 27 per cent only of the enclosures took place in 1578–92, some 61 per cent in 1593–1607 (about 11 per cent being undateable). It is possible, of course, that witnesses tended to bring forward chiefly the most recent cases, but their fading memories of enclosures more than fifteen years old cannot entirely account for the contrasting figures. It seems fairly clear that the Midlands felt enclosure most seriously at the extreme ends of the Tudor period.

It does not seem, incidentally, that the dissolution of the monasteries had a very great effect on the enclosure movement. It is not true that great numbers of peasant farmers, after centuries of kindly treatment by easy-going monastic landlords, were suddenly exposed to ruthless rack-renting and eviction at the hands of the profit-seeking laymen who obtained control of abbey lands in the 1540's and thereafter. The monasteries had not been unworldly and unbusinesslike in the running of their estates, which was in any case often in the hands of lay stewards who were expected to show results. They had not refrained from enclosure—quite the contrary. The inquiry of 1517 showed that in Bedfordshire, Leicestershire and Warwickshire the chances of eviction were about even for tenants on both lay and ecclesiastical estates, while in Berkshire, Northamptonshire and Oxfordshire those on church lands were actually in greater danger during the earlier phase of the movement. In Leicestershire the enclosure carried out by the abbey of Leicester (notably Baggrave

and Ingarsby) prompted the violent attack of Thomas
Rous: "It is a den of thieves and murderers. The profit of
the enclosures the monks enjoy . . . but the voice of the
blood of those slain and mutilated there cries every year to
God for vengeance." No doubt some purchasers of monastic
lands did find them uneconomically run, and sought greater
efficiency by way of enclosure. It is also probably true
that ecclesiastical landlords tended to lease their best lands
rather than run them themselves, while the new landlords
may have preferred direct exploitation. But the weight of
evidence is against the idea that the dissolution provided
a great new impetus to the movement and that the mass of
the English peasantry suffered acutely from the change.

One awkward problem is posed when we place the two
peaks of the enclosure-movement at the beginning and end
of the century. It was suggested that the relatively high
price of wool as compared with grain largely explains the first
peak. But this price-ratio was reversed at the end of the
period, and in theory we should expect a wave of enclosure
for arable farming rather than pasture, and even perhaps the
reconversion of some existing pasture. This does not seem to
have happened in fact. The late-16th century enclosures
continued to aim largely at conversion to pasture, and there
is no substantial evidence of reconversion. How can this be?
A tentative answer may be given when we look at the counties chiefly affected by both peaks, and it is to this problem
of defining the worst-hit areas that we must now turn.

Just as enclosure was not a process that continued at an
even pace throughout the century, so it did not affect all
areas of England equally. The problem was concentrated,
as we have already seen, in some half-dozen counties in the
central Midlands. Other counties were much less afflicted,
either because enclosure had been carried out at a much
earlier date, or because it was unprofitable, or because the
obstacles to it were too great. Regional variations were very
great, and we have to explain not a general phenomenon,
but a localised one, not why the whole English peasantry

suffered, but why one section suffered acutely and why others largely escaped. Contemporaries were perfectly well aware of the localised nature of the problem—the inquiries of 1517, 1548 and 1607 all concentrated mainly on the Midlands—but it has sometimes been lost sight of since.

By the 16th century the Midlands were the classical area of open-field farming. This system was at one time typical of the majority of farming communities of England, and traces of it have been found in nearly every county where soil conditions made it practicable. It was well-suited for the so-called "nucleated village", farming for subsistence rather than for sale, and concerned to distribute arable, meadow and pasture fairly between all the villagers. The arable land was divided into strips representing one day's ploughing, and allocated to the members of the community. It was often, but not always, farmed in a three-field system of rotation, under which one-third was sown with spring corn, one-third with autumn corn, and the remaining third left fallow. Meadow land was likewise divided into strips among the villagers, and after the hay harvest was used for common grazing in the same way that the stubble of the arable fields was grazed after the corn harvest. The commons or waste lands were not divided, though to ensure adequate pasturage for all a stint was sometimes imposed limiting the number of sheep or cattle that each villager might graze upon them. The system had many local variations, both the size of the strips and the cycle of rotation varying with local requirements, and it is dangerous to think too much in terms of a "typical" open-field village. But these broad features could be found in most villages in early medieval England where arable subsistence farming was practised.

It was a system that demanded a high degree of co-operation among the villagers, since all had to sow their strips in the open fields at the same season and all were to some extent dependent on the good-will and efficiency of their neighbours. It was not a highly productive system, and could moreover operate smoothly only in fairly "democratic" communities. Where the incentive of a big market lay close, or where ambitious farmers were steadily building up larger properties by the purchase of their neighbours' strips—and the two tended to go together—the system was likely to break down. Thus Kent, which had long been a granary for London, was reckoned an old-enclosed county by the 16th century. Money rents had appeared there early, and the exceptional freedom that Kentish tenants enjoyed of buying and selling their holdings without licence from the lord of the manor facilitated the consolidation of holdings. Open fields were probably quite common in Kent in the early Middle Ages, but already by the 13th century they were beginning to disappear. Essex likewise felt the pull of the London market, and had in any case substantial areas of woodland and marsh. Enclosure had gone on there also since the 13th century, and the comparatively peaceful enclosures made in the 16th century or later came mainly in the north-west parts of the county adjoining the outer Midlands. Lancashire also seems to have experienced early enclosure, and along with Cheshire, Wiltshire, and the counties of the south-west achieved a balance between arable and pastoral farming that was not upset during the Tudor period. This was no doubt helped in the case of Lancashire and Cheshire by the abundance of good pasture that made conversion and depopulation of arable unnecessary.

In some areas, where the soil was markedly more suitable for either arable or pasture, we would not expect conversion. The reclaimed marshlands of Cambridgeshire, Lincolnshire and the East Riding of Yorkshire consisted of fertile alluvial soil, admirably suited for corn-growing. Here there was no advantage to be gained by conversion to pasture, and it is striking that these areas show no signs of depopulation, no evidence of the Deserted Villages that Maurice Beresford has so assiduously traced in nearly every other district of the kingdom. Equally we could hardly expect the uplands of the West Riding, long devoted to pasture, to change their mode of existence. No market for grain could offer a sufficient inducement towards conversion, nor any ambitious farmer see a profit in it.

In East Anglia, too, the process was largely arrested by the beginning of the Tudor period, though here the enclosures were quite recent in 1485. The Articles of the Norfolk rebels in 1549 contain only one reference to enclosures, and that appears to be in favour of those that have been made for the growing of saffron, a flourishing local industry. In all these areas there might well be complaints of encroachment on the commons, or of their overstocking with the lord's sheep, but not of the depopulating enclosure of arable land. That had already taken place.

What made the Midland counties vulnerable was that the soil over much of their area was equally well adapted for arable or pasture farming. This was not true of the entire area, and neither the wooded districts of Warwickshire south of the Arden nor the Chiltern hills of southern Buckinghamshire were affected by depopulation. But elsewhere the balance between arable and pasture was much more even, and a lively demand for wool could tilt it in favour of the latter. This had happened quite recently in the case of Norfolk, to-day a county of prosperous arable farming. Now the turn of Leicestershire and its neighbours had come. They made up the one major area where conversion could still be made to pay.

Broadly speaking, then, the decisive factor in determining enclosure of arable was its suitability for pastoral farming. There were other more narrowly localized and adventitious factors. Even the greediest and most aggressive landlord could proceed to eviction and enclosure only where the tenants to be displaced were few and vulnerable. Where the freeholders were numerous and the copyholders protected by written deeds or well-attested custom his opportunities were restricted. Thus even within the worst-hit counties the deserted villages tended to be those whose population was already low before the attack developed. Professor Beresford has shown that more than half of 379 lost villages had forty taxpayers or less in 1377. Since the same is true of 1334 also, the Black Death (1348–49) is clearly not a sufficient explanation of their relatively small size, which may have been due to their lying on the poorer soils or to particular local factors that varied from case to case. The smallness is only relative, since at least one-third of them had between 20–40 taxpayers in the 14th century assessments, and were thus not on the very edge of extinction at that date. Moreover some quite sizeable villages were depopulated, while other very small ones survived. But with these qualifications made, Professor Beresford's figures are obviously significant, and it is clear that many village communities suffered because their small size made them vulnerable. The inadequately protected tenure of the villagers in many of them rendered them doubly weak.

This raises the question of who were the villains and who the victims in the enclosure story, and how the former worked their will on the latter. It would be quite false to suggest that all enclosures were the work of great landlords, and that a defenceless peasantry succumbed to them without a struggle. On the contrary, the initiative towards enclosure had often come from small men in the past, and many substantial Tudor yeomen owed their position to peasant ancestors who had patiently built up their holdings by a long process of consolidation and enclosure. That the process could still go on in the Tudor period by peaceful agreement rather than pressure and force is suggested by the absence of friction in such counties as Essex and Sussex, where at least some enclosure continued on a small scale. But it is broadly true to say that in the main Tudor enclosures were enforced from above, and that the class mainly responsible was that loosely but conveniently described as the "squirearchy". In Leicestershire this class carried out nearly 60 per cent of the enclosures made in the years 1485–1550, and over 70 per cent of those in 1551–1607. Their ranks included men who had risen from the peasantry and some of the wealthier yeomen, but the core consisted of gentry families well-established in the county. In the earlier period 18 per cent of the enclosures were effected by the monasteries, and 12 per cent by members of the nobility. In the later period these two elements had faded out (the former as the result of the Dissolution), and the peasantry accounted for 19 per cent of the acreage enclosed. This last significant figure explains, perhaps, why there was little trouble in Leicestershire during the Midlands rising of 1607. The peasants were themselves an important enclosing group. But still only a minority group.

The landlord who wished to enclose had first to dispossess the sitting tenants. If a large number of these were freeholders, he could proceed only with their agreement. Provided they paid rents which were usually nominal and performed certain services—such as infrequent attendance at the manorial court—which were usually little more than nominal, they were perfectly secure in their estates. Those who held of the crown by knight service might still be liable to certain "feudal incidents", of which the most irksome in the Tudor period was wardship—the right of the crown to administer an heir's estate during his minority. But this affected only a minority of freeholders, and in any case did not impair their security of tenure. In the main they were perfectly safe.

The classes vulnerable to enclosure were the copyholders and tenants at will. The copyholders were, broadly speaking, the descendants of villeins on the medieval manors. Villein status, whose distinguishing mark was the performance of labour dues for the lord of the manor, had virtually disappeared by the 16th century, the labour dues having been commuted for money payments that enabled the lord of the manor to work his own demesne by hired labourers. Zealous stewards occasionally still tried to revive them in the Tudor period, but to all intents and purposes labour dues were dead. The tenure of the copyholder varied enormously from one manor to another. Strictly speaking the term only applies to those tenants whose tenure was defined and recorded in the rolls of the court of the manor, and could

2

therefore be said to hold by "copy of the court roll". It is usually applied, however, also to those holding by well-established custom on a manor, though the problem of establishing such custom was itself a material point at issue in Tudor enclosure disputes; only the copyholder whose rights and obligations were in fact recorded on the manor rolls and himself held an authenticated copy of the enrolment was legally in a strong position.

If the copyholder's tenure was a matter of record, there were two further points of crucial concern to him. If he held a "copyhold in inheritance", and could pass his holding to his heir as a matter of right, he was in a strong position and almost as secure as a freeholder. If, however, he held for a term of years only, he was very far from secure, and his position was virtually that of any tenant at will, liable to dispossession when the lease expired. An intermediate position was that of the copyholder who held for life or for "lives"—which usually meant the life of himself, his wife and his next heir. Such a man clearly had more security than the tenant who held for a term of years only, but in the end the lease fell in just the same, and eventually a new bargain had to be struck with the landlord. At this point the would-be encloser could either refuse outright to renew the lease or offer renewal only on impossible terms.

Even if the copyholder held in inheritance, he was not necessarily quite safe. The question then arose whether his payments to the landlord were fixed or uncertain. Rents had quite often been fixed at the time of the commutation of labour dues, and by the 16th century were quite out of step with market rates. Tenants who enjoyed such fixed nominal rents had the advantage of rising food prices without the drawback of rising payments for their land, and were in effect taking an unearned increment from their landlord. But in addition to rent copyholders had also to pay fines, charges payable whenever a leasehold changed hands, usually at the death of the tenant. These were less commonly fixed than were rents, and the landlord who was precluded from rack-renting might thus achieve the same effect by raising fines to an exorbitant level. Up to a point this was a justifiable means of obtaining a reasonable income from his land in 16th century market conditions, but beyond a certain point it could be simply a weapon to obtain the eviction of tenants. Only the copyholder with a sound title, tenure by inheritance, and with fixed rents *and* fines was completely safe.

Available figures are inadequate to say with any certainty (for the country as a whole) how many tenants were freeholders as compared with copyholders, and how many enjoyed reasonable security of tenure. Sample figures collected by R. H. Tawney suggest that copyholders may have made up nearly two-thirds of the whole, and freeholders about one-fifth. But regional variations are very marked indeed. While the Midland counties in the sample produce figures close to the overall ones, Northumberland at one extreme shows a preponderance of over 90 per cent copyholders, while Norfolk and Suffolk produce 36 per cent freeholders. It must be remembered that numerous tenants might hold land in more than one way; yeomen might hold part of their estates in freehold, part in copyhold, and part on short-term leases. In so far as they were copyholders such men were in a much stronger position than those who farmed a small holding on a copyhold tenure only; secure in their freehold estates they could bargain with the landlord on equal terms, and abandon their copyholds and leaseholds if the terms offered were unreasonable. The small copyholder had no such choice; he must accept exorbitant demands or starve.

Sample figures suggest also that more copyholds were held for life or lives than by inheritance, and that fines were more often arbitrary than fixed. This means that a majority of tenants were insecure, and were unprotected at law. Both the Common Law courts and the Court of Chancery gave reasonable protection to the copyholder who could prove the custom of the manor in his favour—provided he had the courage and resources to take his landlord to the courts, as many in fact did. But the majority, who could either prove no good title, or held for a limited term only, or were liable to uncertain fines, were in a very different position. In the last resort they were at the mercy of the enclosing landlord, though the process of their eviction might take time.

To sum up: a substantial number of small farmers were dangerously placed in Tudor England. They were liable to dispossession in those counties where the incentive to enclose was strong, and this was true of the Midlands at the beginning and end of the 16th century. Where enclosure was not the rule, they were liable to rack-renting, arbitrary fines, and the invasion of their rights of pasture on the commons. The intensity of the threat and the degree of security varied enormously from one county to another, and even from one landlord to another. Even a Leicestershire copyhold for life might be safe enough if the landlord were too good-natured or too lazy to seek the greatest profit from his lands. But insecurity was very general, and the copyholders, who formed (as contemporaries agreed) the backbone of agrarian England, could expect only partial and intermittent protection from Tudor governments.

The government was concerned with agrarian problems largely as a matter of public order. There was only one major rising mainly attributable to agrarian discontent—Ket's rebellion in Norfolk in 1549—but others had agrarian elements in them. The destruction of hedges and fences accompanied the Pilgrimage of Grace in 1536 and the Western Rebellion of 1549, though these were chiefly inspired by the government's religious policy. There were some agrarian disturbances in 1569 when the Northern Earls rebelled. Potentially a discontented peasantry was a support for rebels at any time, and a government that depended heavily on local levies for home defence could not afford to alienate the mass of them. This military factor was another argument for government intervention. It was commonly held that shepherds and artisans made poor soldiers, and a thriving peasantry and yeomanry were the backbone of the militia. It was therefore especially undesirable to allow depopulation in strategic areas, and the very first Tudor statute against depopulation (1488) emphasized this danger in the Isle of Wight. An allied consideration was the desire to make England self-supporting in time of war, and for this end it was necessary to maintain tillage and avoid dependence on imports of foreign grain. Even in time of peace a bad harvest might mean severe local famines, and if the government hoped to control the price of food it must logically also try to ensure supplies. The maintenance of tillage and the avoidance of depopulation went hand in hand.

The government also had a financial stake in the problem. An important source of revenue was the subsidy on incomes from land, and so ill-adjusted was the scale of assessment that the wealthier landlords escaped very lightly. A concentration of more land in fewer hands meant loss of income to the Crown, as well as being politically undesirable. In so far as enclosure was the work of the greater landlords, this supplied another motive for intervention.

Some weight must also be given to more idealistic motives. The crown undoubtedly recognized a duty of safeguarding its subjects' livelihood. It also was moved by the conservative ideal of maintaining the social structure as it was, of preserving the balance between social classes. This meant protecting peasant as well as noble in the status to which it pleased Providence to call them. In the mid-century the government, in the person of Protector Somerset, was powerfully moved by the advocacy of the preachers—Latimer, Lever, Crowley and others—and of the layman John Hales, who eloquently denounced the avarice of landlords and demanded justice for the poor. The advocacy of this group, sometimes called the "Commonwealth party", partly explains the paradox of government action against enclosures at a date when enclosure was least in evidence. Such arguments did not appeal to the hard-headed businessmen who surrounded Somerset in the Council, but they gained a brief ascendancy in 1548 and were not wholly ineffective at other times.

Government action was partly expressed in legislation. The 1488 Act for the Isle of Wight, aimed primarily at the evil of engrossing, was followed by a general Act in 1489 aimed at the twin evil of depopulation. This process had gone so far, the preamble alleged, that:

> where in some towns two hundred persons were occupied and lived by their lawful labours, now be there occupied two or three herdsmen and the residue fall in idleness, thus husbandry which is one of the greatest commodities of this realme is greatly decayed, churches destroyed, the service of God withdrawn, the bodies there buried and not prayed for, the patron and curates wronged, the defence of this land against our enemies outwards feebled and impaired, to the great displeasure of God, to the subversion of the policy and good rule of this land, and [if] remedy be not hastily therefore purveyed.

There is no evidence that either of these acts was enforced. The same is true of an act of 1515, which sought to prevent conversion of arable to pasture and the consequent shortage of grain, but optimistically left enforcement to the landlords. An act of 1536 more realistically put the initiative into the King's hands, and this time action did follow. Meanwhile the problem was also being attacked from another angle in an attempt to make sheep-farming less attractive and profitable. In 1533 an act laid down that no man might keep a flock of more than 2,400 sheep, and the same idea inspired the brief-lived poll-tax on sheep and a new tax on cloth in 1549; a census of sheep was attempted in 1549, but no money seems to have come in, and the act was repealed the following year. The latter half of the century was not marked by much agrarian legislation (or agitation). The policy of encouraging the export of corn, begun in 1563, may have raised its price and helped to discourage enclosure. But the experiment of repealing much of the anti-enclosure legislation in 1593 did not prove a success; it allegedly led to a new wave of enclosure, and was reversed in 1597. It is possible that the government was unduly influenced by the bad harvests of the intervening years, which were enough on their own to cause a sharp increase of grain-prices.

The crucial problem was not a legislative one, however, except in so far as it was difficult to pass effective acts in a parliament composed largely of landowners. Enforcement was the real issue, and the government's efforts were only intermittent. Two major commissions of inquiry were held, the first, initiated by Wolsey, in 1517, and the second, that of John Hales, in 1548. The former collected a substantial amount of information over a wide area; the latter produced a little information from a few Midland counties, and aroused local riots into the bargain. Neither can be said to have elicited convincing evidence of large-scale enclosure, and the fault was probably in the terms of reference given to the commissions rather than pressure from landlords or intimidation of juries. The 1517 commission looked back as far as 1488; since it found relatively few enclosures of more than 100 acres the inference is that such enclosures had mainly taken place before 1488. Hales himself admitted that his commission had come too late, and that the major offences were already long-standing. The information that the government obtained was thus only of limited value.

Government action based on this information tended to be short-lived and rather ineffective. The Star Chamber and Court of Requests did deal with a steady trickle of cases, the former being especially concerned where public order had been threatened. To the Exchequer Court came a number of cases arising from breaches of statutes, and there were two short periods of intensive activity there in 1518–19 and 1539–42. These continued even during the régime of the Duke of Northumberland (1549–53), which saw also a statute against conversion of arable to pasture. But offenders were often lightly dealt with, the government sometimes contenting itself with mere promises to make amends, and these cases leave a strong impression that the big fish escaped the net. Action had come too late, and was difficult to sustain. Though Tudor monarchs and their councils were well able to enforce their will in urgent and grave matters, it was virtually impossible to enforce over a long period a policy directly contrary to the interests of the landed classes. To keep the general support of those who ran the counties tacit concessions had to be made.

Did it really matter that government intervention achieved so little—beyond perhaps slowing down the tempo of the enclosure movement? Was the problem, in fact, as pressing as government and pamphleteers imagined, or has its importance been greatly exaggerated? The extent of known 16th century enclosures is certainly unimpressive—less than three per cent of the most seriously affected counties—and it is well-known, of course, that much land waited till the 18th century to become enclosed. But the bare figures do not fairly reflect the impact on contemporary society. Much more than three per cent of the *cultivable* land was affected, though we cannot estimate the exact proportion. In Leicestershire one village in three was struck by enclosure, even if only two were totally enclosed, and this clearly represents a great deal of local disturbance and hardship. In a much less mobile society than our own the evicted peasant could not easily find new employment, and small disturbances of the economy had much more dire consequences. Even a very small enclosure might disastrously impede access to pasturage. We may feel that the government's efforts were mistimed, and that the great problems of the mid-century were rack-renting and encroachment on commons rather than enclosure. We have no right to say that these efforts were wholly mistaken, or belittle the sufferings of the victims.

With this said, it remains difficult to say why the matter was so debated in 1548–49, and to show what the real grievances were at that time. Some suggestions may be found in the articles of complaint presented by the Norfolk rebels of 1549. These barely mention enclosures, except to ask that legislation against them should not be enforced against those who have made them for the growing of saffron, an important local industry. The main agrarian grievances are two-fold: there is powerful feeling against rack-renting, and an optimistic wish that rents should be fixed at the level of 1485, and that only an "easy fine" should be exacted at the death of a tenant or the sale of copyhold land; there are also complaints of loss of common rights, and equally optimistic wishes that lords of manors should not pasture their beasts upon the commons at all and that no lord or gentleman with more than forty pounds a year from his estates should graze any bullocks or sheep anywhere. There are numerous other grievances implied, including an interesting suggestion that information on the laws to protect poor men's rights has been hidden by the local authorities, and the famous demand "that all bond men may be made free, for God made all free with his precious blood shedding." The former of these is of doubtful validity, and the latter of little relevance at a time when villein status had virtually disappeared. Commons and rents were the chief matters of concern. Other factors not specifically mentioned were the debasement of the currency and consequent inflation of the 1540's, and the belief that Protector Somerset was in sympathy with the rebels' aims. It was the fatal delusion that the Council as a whole might support Somerset in his policy of agrarian reform that encouraged Ket and his followers to set up their orderly armed camp outside Norwich, to refuse pardon on the grounds that they had done no wrong, and when sharp disillusionment followed to fight the pitched battle of Dusindale, where they were cut down by the Earl of Warwick and his German mercenaries. Their rebellion gave Warwick and his supporters in the Council grounds for overthrowing Somerset, and the partial abandonment (not a total reversal) of his policy.

How far were the grievances of the Norfolk rebels justified, and how far were they typical of other counties? Overstocking of the commons was a recurrent complaint, and in Norfolk was sometimes combined with abuse of the foldcourse system—a specifically Norfolk institution that provided for the pasturage of sheep and the manuring of the arable fields

2*

by the co-operation of both lord and tenants. (Abuses of it are surprisingly not mentioned in the "articles" of 1549.) A great sheep-farmer like Thomas Townshend, who had some 4000 sheep in West Norfolk in the 1540's, found pasture for them by ruthlessly pushing out his competitors. In Norfolk such practices were limited by the large number of free-holders and protected copyholders. In the north and west tenants were in a weaker position, and where pasturage was scarce the abuse was likely to be the more prevalent. Un-fortunately we are ill-informed as to its extent, since no government inquiry was specifically devoted to it, and it was less likely than enclosure to become the subject of court cases. But it is probably safe to assume that it was wide-spread in sheep-farming counties, and may often have been a more real grievance than the much-publicised enclosures. It was as effective a way of evicting unwanted tenants, and had the advantage of being legal.

Similarly we are inadequately informed about the extent of rack-renting in Norfolk or the country as a whole. Sample figures from Wiltshire, based on accounts of the Herbert and Seymour estates, suggest that some increases of rent were quite spectacular. Rents per acre on new takings on the Herbert manors increased more than five-fold in the course of the century, those on the Seymour estates nearly nine-fold. Fines, here and elsewhere, followed a similar course, and because they were less often fixed than rents might rise even higher. Since these increased charges could only be levied on new takings, the landlord's total income did not rise in the same proportion. But since in these quoted in-stances rents were rising much more rapidly than prices, hard-headed landlords could at least keep pace with any increased expenses they had to face. Less forceful landlords—among whom the crown was prominent—might grant long leases on generous terms; some sample crown manors show rent increases of only 50 per cent during the century. Such modest increases suggest either that the landlord was in a poor bargaining position or that he refrained for political and social reasons from upsetting his tenants. Or, again, he might simply be unbusinesslike. The numbers and proportion of harsh and lenient landlords is quite impossible to determine in the present imperfect state of our knowledge. But the fiery denunciations of the "greedy cormorants" by Crowley and the other Commonwealth men suggest considerable hardship.

In part the protests were unjustified, however understandable. Many copyhold and leasehold tenants had long enjoyed the benefit of rising prices for farm products and stationary rents. They had thus, in a sense, profited at the expense of their landlords, and their position was analogous to that of many household tenants under the protection of the 20th century Rent Acts. It was not unreasonable for landlords to try to adjust rents to rising prices, and to secure a share in the increased profits of farming. Some enhancement of rents was only to be expected. It is quite understandable, on the other hand, that men who had long enjoyed security and low rents should resent increases and the threat of eviction. They felt morally entitled to their privileged position in the same way that some tenants in 1962 feel morally obliged to pay only 1939 rents. It is also fair to say that the changes were too sudden and too extreme. In both the 16th and 20th centuries a great and rapid increase in rents constituted a legitimate grievance. Government action to limit it would have been quite reasonable and more helpful than their ineffective attempts to halt enclosures. But in 16th century conditions a comprehensive system of rent-control was hardly to be looked for.

It is still not clear why discontent should have reached a peak in 1548–49. Possibly the inflation of the 1540's accelerated rack-renting, though the Herbert and Seymour accounts do not support this idea, and show a marked increase in the following decade. Perhaps the distress and insecurity caused by inflation prompted men to examine all other possible grievances, and to rake up those of long-standing as well as those of immediate relevance. It is difficult otherwise to account for the special attention devoted to enclosures at this date. Local and personal factors no doubt also played their part. The Norfolk rebellion was triggered off by a local disturbance that had several precedents in earlier years; perhaps we should ask ourselves why these led to no major upheaval rather than why that of 1549 did. The temporary influence of the Commonwealth men was partly a political accident; their conservatism led them to look too much to the past in their analysis of contemporary distress. At all events it seems likely that the period of most active government concern for agrarian problems did not coincide with the period of most intensive enclosure, and that Somerset and his advisers concentrated on the wrong problem.

For all that agrarian disorders and misdeeds bulk large in the literature of the time, it would be a mistake to regard the Tudor period as one of widespread revolutionary change in agriculture. Certainly the pull of the urban markets grew more pronounced, but even at the end of the 16th century a Leicestershire village like Wigston Magna was still practising a primarily subsistence economy. Only those areas enjoying good communications with London and other cities were very much affected as yet. Much of the Midlands had no very easy commercial outlet, and this may explain the paradox that while enclosures took place for conversion to pasturage in the early years of the century (when wool prices were relatively high) there was no reconversion of pasture to arable in the last decades of the century (when grain prices soared). The farms of Kent and Essex, and the market gardens of the Home Counties, were not yet patterns for the whole of England.

Nor were the lives of the majority of English peasants turned upside down. A minority suffered acutely, but most were governed by the rhythm of the seasons and the vagaries of the English climate far more than by the avarice of landlords. Those who escaped the hazards of rack-renting and eviction benefited from high prices at the end of the century, and these are reflected in the longer and richer inventories left by even the humbler small farmers of late-Elizabethan England.

There were no great accessions of new territory brought under the plough. The draining of the Fens was planned before the end of Elizabeth's reign, but the addition of half a million acres of arable land came with the first Stuarts. The Tudor age saw only slow accretions, such as those of the Lincolnshire coast. No important new crops were developed, and the Leicestershire farmers continued to sow their fields with peas, beans and barley, with wheat and rye occupying only a small proportion of the acreage sown—$12\frac{1}{2}$ per cent in 1588. (It is important to remember that wheat was not the staple grain of Tudor England, and that wheat prices are therefore a far from satisfactory index of prosperity and living-standards.) In Leicestershire the proportion of wheat and rye sown actually fell during the 16th century. Systems of crop-rotation, though by no means uniform over the whole country, were marked by local diversity rather than experiment and innovation.

Some advances were, however, made. The manuring of fields was more intensive and widespread. The use of lime was well-established by 1600, and marl was not uncommon —in spite of the fears of some tenant-farmers that their rents would be raised if they increased the fertility of their holdings. From the Golden Vale of Hereford and the Wylye Valley in Wiltshire developed the practice of floating water-meadows; this produced a richer grass crop than was otherwise possible. It cannot be said that Tudor fertilising was very scientific; 16th century scientists were too preoccupied with the idea of discovering a single vital salt which would work agricultural magic. But the practical common-sense of the farmers was a sounder basis for action, and their hard work brought results. Whereas the best 13th century farms had produced only 6–12 bushels to the acre, the Elizabethan farmer could expect at least 16. This increased productivity was not due only to administrative changes through the consolidation of holdings and economies in labour.

Books to advise the Tudor farmer appeared in increasing numbers as the century wore on. The first was Sir Anthony Fitzherbert's *Book of Husbandry*, which appeared in 1523. It went through a number of editions before 1600, which shows that its shrewd and sensible advice over the whole range of arable farming was much appreciated at the time; it has also proved an invaluable source to historians, who have used it as first-hand evidence of contemporary farming practice. Even more popular was Thomas Tusser's *A hundred good points of husbandry* (1557), expanded to five hundred points in 1573, and of which four more editions appeared up to 1593. It was written in verse that sometimes rises above mere doggerel, and told the farmer how to conduct his family life as well as his farm. It is sad to record that Tusser did not make a success of his Suffolk farm, and found authorship too brought meagre rewards:

> My music since hath been the plough
> Entangled with, some care among:
> The gain not great, the pain enough
> Hath made me sing another song.

The Four Books of Husbandry of Barnaby Googe (1577), in the main a translation, brought to the attention of English farmers the more advanced practices of the Dutch—in particular the growing of turnips as winter feed for livestock, a perennial problem of 16th century farming. Less helpfully, he also offered advice on the growing of olives. More specialised works appeared on the care of horses, bees, hop-gardens and flowers. The Tudor farmer certainly did not suffer from want of instruction.

How far he could or would avail himself of it is another matter. The advice of the text-book writers was not uniformly sound and useful. With much that was practical it included also a great deal of borrowing from classical authors (and more unacknowledged borrowing from contemporaries) with much irrelevance and unscientific nonsense. To follow *all* the counsel offered would not have led to a fortune, and Tusser was not a good advertisement for his own wares. Discriminating readers could, however, follow Sir Hugh Plat's sensible advice on manures while ignoring his exaggerated claims for the practice of setting corn seed at equal distances apart. But the number of such readers cannot have been great in spite of the apparent demand for Fitzherbert, Tusser and Googe; Tudor editions were numerous but small. The theorists wrote for a restricted audience at best, and it would be hard to prove their influence even on these. No eager cultivation of turnips followed immediately on the appearance of Googe's work. Progress in agriculture was essentially empirical, and much more to the point was Googe's precept that "good ffarming was where the master frequently manured his ground with his foot and provendered his larder with his eye."

For those who escaped the dangers of eviction and rack-renting, and who followed this advice, farming afforded at least a modest subsistence and at best a comfortable prosperity. Great profits went, no doubt, to the rack-renter rather than the hard-working farmer, but both enjoyed a rising standard of living at the end of Elizabeth's reign. The land offered a hard and active life, and the hazards of weather and disease made it an uncertain one too. But contemporaries were not wholly mistaken in regarding it as more solid and rewarding than other occupations. Even the Northamptonshire copyholder might be safer than the Wiltshire weaver in time of trade crisis, or the London mason in a year of famine.

II

OVERSEAS TRADE

THE LATER SIXTEENTH CENTURY saw great changes in both the character and direction of England's overseas trade, though these were not as contentious as the changes in agrarian life. The most obvious of them can be seen in the new trading companies which sprang up in Elizabeth's reign and which enormously extended the geographical range of Tudor merchant acitivity. Less immediately striking, but of great long-term importance, was the development of a more diversified export trade and of new forms of commercial organisation. Taken together these changes have led some historians to view the Elizabethan age as one of general expansion and confident prosperity. No doubt there is some truth in this idea, but the expansion can easily be exaggerated; it was territorial rather than quantitative, and the changes of kind rather than of degree. This does not, of course, diminish the interest and importance of these changes, and of the marked contrast between the first half of the century and the second. It is the aim of this chapter to explain and discuss them.

Throughout the whole Tudor period England's export trade was dominated by a single commodity—woollen cloth. English wool had long been famous, of course, but in earlier centuries had been exported in its raw state, to be worked by Flemish and Italian weavers. In the decade 1350–1360 wool exports had averaged as much as 32,000 sacks a year, with each sack containing (officially) 364 pounds of wool. Cloth exports at that time amounted to only 5000 a year. Already by the end of the 14th century the balance had greatly changed, and in the years 1390–99 some 19,000 sacks of wool were exported annually as against 37,000 cloths. The trend continued throughout the 15th century, and by the end of Henry VII's reign a bare 5000 sacks of wool were shipped abroad each year, while cloth exports had reached 82,000, and were to rise to 118,000 in the years 1538–44. In this latter period raw wool accounted for only 8 per cent, woollen cloth for 92 per cent, of the value of the total trade—an almost exact reversal of the proportions of 1350–60. A revolution had taken place.

All these dry figures are taken from official customs accounts. For the purposes of the customer it was presumed that there existed a standard broadcloth in terms of which all kinds of woollen cloth could be counted, and statutes periodically laid down the official length and breadth of this unit. This was simply a convenient fiction. In fact there was no such standardised article, and probably few cloths conformed strictly to the official dimensions. These may well have laid down the minimum length and breadth, but cloths might measure as much as 30 or even 45 yards in length, and not merely the statutory 24. Moreover, all manner of other woollen cloths were reckoned as broadcloths to suit the customer's convenience: there was a recognised scale of conversion that rated three kerseys or six "dozens" as equal to one broadcloth, and similarly for other lesser varieties. The official figures therefore obscure the rich variety of English woollens in the 16th century, and exaggerate the importance of the broadcloth. The smaller and lighter kerseys may well have accounted for nearly a third of the cloth exports of Henry VIII's reign, and the coarse "dozens" of Yorkshire and Devon, the Welsh friezes, and the "cottons" of Lancashire and Cheshire were at least useful as wrappers in which to ship the more valuable clothes.

Most broadcloths—and we must use the term, if only to distinguish them from the lighter woollens—came from the West Country, especially from Gloucestershire, Somerset and above all Wiltshire. Some special varieties, such as "Worcesters" and "Castlecombes" had a European reputation, though by the 16th century the names probably indicated a type of cloth rather than the actual place of origin. Most of them were exported in an undyed state, to be finished by Flemish experts for critical foreign buyers. The English cloth-finishing industry had a poor reputation abroad, and our merchants found they could sell the unfinished product more profitably. This was contrary to government policy, and successive statutes in 1487, 1512, 1514 and 1536 made it an offence to ship unfinished cloth below stipulated price-levels. But merchants cheerfully evaded the statutes, and the price-levels for the export of unfinished cloth were raised from time to time in such a way that only a minority of the dearer cloths were in fact affected. Those English broadcloths that were dyed at home came for the most part from East Anglia and Kent, areas which seem to have specialised in high-quality cloths that were coloured blue, green, russet, violet or red (with blue predominating) before being sent across the seas.

While broadcloths found their customers mainly in Germany and the Netherlands, the lighter and finer kerseys found their way also to Italy and the Levant. The best quality ones came largely from Berkshire, where Newbury was a celebrated centre for their production. Unlike the broadcloths they were very frequently dyed before export. They appear to have maintained their reputation rather better than the broadcloths, since when complaints of the quality of English cloth became common in the 1540's and 1550's these were almost entirely confined to the heavier cloths. The cheaper kerseys came chiefly from the West Riding of Yorkshire and Devon, and were usually exported undyed.

Other varieties of woollens were relatively insignificant in the export trade. In a big shipment of cloth to Antwerp in 1535 broadcloths and kerseys between them accounted for 95 per cent of the total, the kerseys alone amounting to 30 per cent. In brief, it is fair to say that English exports in the 16th century consisted largely of West Country broadcloths and Berkshire kerseys, and that the wealth of the great London merchants rested on the sustained efforts of several generations of weavers in some five or six counties.

Wool, of course, continued to be shipped to Calais, where since the 14th century the staple for it had been fixed. But since the 14th century also the wool trade had been the milch-cow of a needy royal exchequer, and it is hardly too much to say that it was taxed out of existence. In 1485 the custom on wool amounted to nearly one-third of its value, while that on cloth was in the region of three per cent. This clearly gave the cloth-exporters a decisive advantage over the merchants of the Staple of Calais, and the latter were further involved in heavy commitments in paying for the English garrison in Calais. Failure to meet these commitments incurred the royal wrath and yet further expenditure —it cost the Staplers £20,000 to make their peace with Henry VIII after defaulting on their 1515 contract—and thus still further reduced their resources for the purchase of supplies in England. These supplies dwindled as the growing cloth industry at home absorbed more and more of the available wool, while at the same time foreign demand slackened as English competition began to put the Flemish weavers out of business. These factors are quite enough to explain the decline of the wool trade, to which the loss of Calais in 1558 was a further blow. The crafty Italians, shipping wool direct to the Mediterranean under royal licence, had little to do with the case, for all the anguished complaints of the Staplers at the time.

Some other goods were exported too—the tin of Devon and Cornwall, whether in its raw state or manufactured into pewter. An insignificant quantity of leather also still found its way abroad, and corn might be exported when the harvest had been exceptionally good. But wool and woollens accounted for about four-fifths of the value of English exports in Henry VIII's reign, and the whole foreign trade was thus dangerously dependent on the good health of a single industry.

Imports were very much more varied. Some of them were raw materials for English industry, such as the iron which was an important product of Spain at this time. From Spain also came oil and soap that could be used in the cloth industry as well as for domestic purposes, while the famous woad of Toulouse along with madder and alum from the Antwerp market could also be considered as essentials for the native cloth-finishers. Some imported manufactures might also be considered as essentials, or at least cannot fairly be put in the category of luxuries. The fustians of South Germany (coarse cloths of cotton, or wool and cotton mixed) and the linens of France and the Netherlands might clothe English soldiers and apprentices, and certainly bulked large in the customers' accounts. But a high proportion of imported wares in this period can have been of interest only to the wealthier classes. The wines of Gascony and Spain, the pepper, ginger and sugar bought of Portuguese agents at Antwerp, were not consumed by peasants. Nor were the copper kettles and pans from Bavaria likely to be found in humble homes, and the only "essential" item among fairly substantial imports of metal-ware was the armour that was brought in when foreign governments from time to time permitted its export. Also non-essential, in a strict sense, was the vast quantity of haberdashery of all kinds—hats, caps, bonnets, gloves, ribbons, pins, needles, beads, buckles, brooches and so forth—that poured in every year. This was no doubt more widely distributed than the luxury silks and velvets of Italy, also a major item, but gave rise to the objection that its import put native craftsmen out of work.

Many contemporaries, indeed, took an austere view of imports to England in this period, mainly for this reason. In the *Discourse of the Common Weal of this Realm of England*, an imaginary conversation on economic affairs composed in 1549, the Doctor is made to say:

> And I marvel no man taketh head unto it, what number first of trifles cometh hither from beyond the seas, that we might either clean spare, or else make them within our own Realm, for the which we pay inestimable treasure every year, or else exchange substantial wares and necessary for them, for the which we might receive great treasure. Of the which sort I mean glasses, dials, tables, cards, balls, puppets, penhorns, inkhorns, toothpicks, gloves, knives, daggers, pouches, brooches, aiglets, buttons of silk and silver, earthen pots, pins, points, hawks' bells, paper both white and brown, and a thousand like things, ... And as for some things, they make it or our own commodities and send it us again, whereby they set their people on work, and do exhaust much treasure out of this Realm. As of our wool they make cloth, caps, and kersies; of our fells [leather] they make Spanish skins, gloves, girdles; of our tin, salts [saltcellars] spoons and dishes, of our broken linen, cloth and rags,

paper both white and brown. What treasure, think you, goeth out of this Realm for every of these things? And then for all together it exceedeth my estimation.

This argument is not as sensible as the author would have us believe. It may well be true that some English craftsmen suffered from the competition, but it is quite likely that at least some of the foreign wares were better-made, and not merely more fashionable. It is not self-evident that native workers deserved to be artificially protected from their overseas rivals. Nor is there any evidence that there was indeed an abundance of untapped "treasure", whether in the form of raw materials or specie—and export of the latter was in any case restricted by foreign governments. In the absence of this treasure the English merchant had to take what he could get on the foreign market and sell on the home market; equally foreigners could not buy our cloth if we did not take their goods in exchange. The moralist might deplore the frivolity of his fellow-countrymen, but to argue like the Doctor was to ignore hard economic realities.

England's foreign trade in the early 16th century, therefore, consisted in the exchange of cloth for a variety of foreign wares. It seems clear from the evidence of private merchants' accounts that the profits of this trade were made on the sale of the cloth abroad, rather than on the sale of the imports at home. Cloth could be sold in Antwerp in the 1520's and 1530's at a gross profit of 20–25 per cent, but the goods brought home added little if anything to the merchant's gains. Private and national prosperity rested on the continuing sale of a single commodity.

Not only was trade thus narrowly based; it was also heavily concentrated in a single port—London. This was already the case in 1485, and during the first six years of Henry VII's reign 70 per cent of England's cloth exports passed through the capital. A boom in Southampton's trade in the last years of the reign temporarily reversed the trend, but by the end of Henry VIII's reign as much as 88 per cent of the cloth exports were shipped at London. Figures for other commodities show a similar development. This had not seemed inevitable at the outset, and for the first few years of Henry VII's reign the other ports of the realm had shared in a general recovery after the late-15th century depression. A turning-point can be seen about 1500, after which date the trade of London continued to increase, while that of the out-ports declined not only relatively but absolutely, and they were left far behind. Throughout the Tudor period bitter jealousy existed between London and the provincial ports, jealousy inspired partly by the simple fact of London's ascendancy, partly by the deliberately exclusive policy that the rich London merchants adopted towards their less fortunate rivals.

The ascendancy was only in part due to geographical advantages. London was well-placed to exploit both the old-established trade-routes to the Baltic and the newly developing Atlantic ones. It was also near to Antwerp, the centre of European trade in the early 16th century. But other ports were scarcely less well-situated, and these factors alone would not explain London's remarkable pre-eminence. London, however, was more than just a port; it was also the political capital, the centre of government and administration. The court became increasingly fixed in or near London, while the chief law-courts of the kingdom were also to be found there. Courtiers and a swelling throng of litigants added to the industrial and commercial population, and an active land- and marriage-market brought rich gentlemen looking for a good investment and poor ones looking for a wealthy wife. Business attracted more business, and once London's lead was established a "snowball" process made it all the more marked and secure. It was not surprising that provincial merchants tended to migrate to London, while the Italians forsook Southampton and the Hansards left Kingston-upon-Hull to seek better contacts and richer opportunities.

It is possible to exaggerate the extent of London's predominance. Customs accounts deal only with overseas trade, and therefore do not fairly reflect the activity of ports concerned mainly in the coastal trade. Newcastle, developing its coal exports to London, is not fairly represented. The customs accounts have the further disadvantage that for obvious reasons they do not record the smuggling trade, a very real if hidden economic activity. This was undoubtedly greater in the outports, where there were fewer customs officials to bribe, intimidate or coerce, and where sturdy local feeling (and therefore local juries) could be relied upon to stand firm against the agents and informers of the central government. But with these qualifications made, it can hardly be disputed that London controlled the bulk of England's trade, and that in the economic as well as the political sense "Tudor despotism" consisted in London's dominance over the rest of the country.

Just as London was the single funnel through which cloth-exports poured, so Antwerp was in the first half of the 16th century the immediate destination of the greater part of them. Antwerp had recently inherited the position just vacated by Bruges, that of the greatest port of northern Europe. It was more favourably placed than the Flemish city to exploit the growing trade of the merchants of South Germany. It had had the tact not to quarrel with the new Habsburg overlords of the Netherlands, as both Bruges and Ghent had not. But most important of all, Antwerp became the effective staple for the most sought-after commodities of European trade. It became a main centre of the spice trade with the arrival of the Portuguese royal factor in 1494. The South German merchants brought their silver, copper and fustians—the first being an especial attraction for the Portuguese, who need it to buy their spices in the Far East. Alum, the essential mordant in the cloth-dyeing industry, was officially stapled at Antwerp, and had an importance out of all proportion to the quantities handled. But by far the most important single commodity concentrated at Antwerp was English cloth itself; a contemporary estimated that it accounted for nearly a third of all imports to the city, and the English merchants had some reason for thinking that they could make or break the prosperity of Antwerp and that their withdrawal would be a disastrous blow. Thus all merchants who sought English cloth, Portuguese spices, German copper or papal alum had to come to Antwerp to get it, and in their turn brought other wares—Italian silks, French and Spaniah wines, Netherlands linens and grain from the Baltic—which together made Antwerp the greatest mart of Europe.

The financiers followed the merchants, the two callings being often combined in any case in this period. South German firms like the Fugger, Welser and Hochstetter of Augsburg, and Italian ones like the Affaitadi of Cremona, had their permanent agents there, most of them well-established by 1510. In 1531 the city built a celebrated new Bourse, the model for London's Royal Exchange. Here the merchants and exchange-dealers met daily to do their commercial and financial business, and within a few decades Antwerp was the greatest financial centre of Europe as well as its greatest market.

The foreigners in Antwerp formed permanent communities, often with their own officials and residences. The English and Portuguese were the best organised and closest-knit, but the Spanish and Italians also formed distinct groups with recognized status and privileges. On the other hand the South Germans were not so fully organised or numerous, though the importance of firms such as the Fugger and Welser clearly cannot be measured by mere numbers. The Hansards, though individually active in the city, did not take up corporate residence there till 1569, and then the great days of Antwerp were already over. All foreigners enjoyed a freedom from restrictions that was unusual by 16th century standards. The "modernity" of the city's atmosphere must not be exaggerated, but Antwerp was free from the xenophobia that disgraced London in the riots of Evil May Day in 1517.

The greatness of Antwerp covered a span of some thirty

years, from about 1520 to 1550. But its foundations were insecure, since it depended so much on the continued flow of goods brought by the foreigners, and the continued presence of the foreigners within its walls. Its own cloth-finishing industry, its printing works, the enterprise of native Antwerp merchants who traded extensively with Spain and ventured on occasion to the New World and to India—all these were not sufficient security. When depression struck the English cloth trade and the Portuguese spice trade in the 1550's, when the great German merchant-bankers were shattered by the Habsburg bankruptcy of 1556, and when religious persecution began in earnest with the "placards" of 1555, then the flow of goods that had constituted Antwerp's attractive force dried up and the merchants of Protestant countries felt themselves insecure. If a single turning-point must be sought, then the English cloth crisis of 1551 is as appropriate as any. The Spanish Fury of 1576, when Requesens' mutinous troops destroyed so much of the city, the closure of the Scheldt by the northern rebels in 1585 (cutting Antwerp off from the open sea) were further heavy blows. But twenty years before 1576 the greatness of Antwerp was already on the wane. After 1585 it was a thing of the past.

Obviously Antwerp was not the only foreign port frequented by English merchants. London, Southampton and Bristol all had well-established connections with Spain, and in the early years of the 16th century this trade continued active. Small groups of merchants were established at several Spanish ports, especially at Seville, the most flourishing of them, men like the London Draper Thomas Howell, whose ledger for the years 1522–27 has survived. One such colony was active at San Lucar de Barrameda, at the mouth of the Guadalquivir, where the Duke of Medina-Sidonia showed special favour to the English, and where from 1530 their community held a special grant from Henry VIII as the Andalusia Company. Merchants who seldom visited Spain in person might well employ resident factors, who frequently worked on a commission basis, receiving $2\frac{1}{2}$ per cent from their principals on the business done in their name. In the first decades of the century English visitors and residents continued to be quite numerous.

Trade and visitors tended to fall away towards the middle of the century for a number of reasons. Henry VIII's break with Rome brought his subjects into conflict with the Inquisition, and several English merchants had reason to complain of petty and even major vexations. One Thomas Pery had a long tale to tell of persecutions suffered in 1538–39, which culminated in six months' imprisonment and forfeiture of goods—all for maintaining, so he said, that Henry VIII was a good Christian. It is likely that those English merchants who acted and spoke with reasonable discretion escaped the attentions of the Inquisition, but it is clear that friction was mounting from the 1530's onwards and that the English merchants felt themselves increasingly insecure. Tension was not lessened by acts of violence committed at sea by English sea-captains, though it is possible that some of these may have been inspired by the Inquisition. The most sensational of these was the seizure, in 1545, of the treasure-ship *San Salvador* by Robert Reneger, a displeasing feature of this from the Spanish viewpoint being that Reneger, like Drake in 1580, was well-received at the English court when he brought his booty home. In the following year, 1546, Spanish shipping was attacked within the north-east port of Munguia. Already before the end of Henry VIII's reign the atmosphere was beginning to resemble that of Elizabeth's. Since during this period Bristol and Southampton were both losing ground to London, and London was tending to concentrate its trade increasingly on Antwerp, it is hardly surprising that a combination of such religious, political and economic factors brought about a marked decline in Anglo-Spanish trade.

Trade with the Mediterranean was active in the first years of the century. For a short time indeed, this brought about a revival in the fortunes of Southampton, which from the mid-fifteenth century had suffered from the gradual disappearance of Venetian and Genoese merchants at its wharves. During Henry VII's reign an increasing taste for Mediterranean luxuries, especially malmsey wine, and firm diplomatic backing by the king, encouraged English merchants to develop their trade with Pisa (a subject city of Florence) in the west and the island of Chios in the east. In the last two years of the reign poundage was paid on over £100,000 worth of goods at Southampton. But by the middle of the century most of this activity had ceased. English shipping became more and more liable to attack by Turkish forces and the Algerian corsairs in league with them; the last major venture, that of the *Aucher* to Chios in 1552, ended in precipitate flight to escape destruction. By this date, moreover, much English cloth passed southwards through Antwerp along the safer overland route over the Alps. The risks of the Mediterranean sea-trade were only doubtfully worth running. So by the mid-century a second sphere of activity was closing to English merchants. Southampton, after a period in which London merchants used it for their southern trade and made it an economic suburb of the capital, became a decayed port that waited till the 19th century for its revival.

England had always traded substantially with the Baltic, which unlike the Mediterranean supplied her with essential raw materials such as timber, wax, tar and hemp, all vital for the ship-building industry. In return the cities of northern Germany took large quantities of English woollen cloth. But in the late Middle Ages most of this trade had been in the hands of the Hanseatic League, which in the 15th century was strong enough to exclude English merchants from any effective share in the Baltic trade. Their victory had been sealed in 1474 by the Treaty of Utrecht, where thanks in part to their help in restoring Edward IV to the throne in 1471, they obtained extensive privileges in England without offering any comparable ones to their rivals at home. Thus while the Hansards paid only one shilling on each broadcloth exported (as against 1s. 2d. payable by Englishmen) and did not pay the subsidy of a shilling in the pound on general commodities at all, and while they enjoyed also a privileged position in their Steelyard in London, English merchants at Danzig had no comparable privileges and exemptions and traded at a serious disadvantage. There was much friction between English and Hansards throughout the reigns of Henry VII and Henry VIII, and neither king was able to gain material concessions for his subjects. The Hansards continued to handle nearly one-quarter of England's cloth exports and effectively monopolised the Baltic trade. Whether they willed or no the English were forced to resort to Antwerp as their one major outlet in northern Europe.

Some trade also took place with France, although that country remained the principal political rival and enemy of England for the first half of the century. The old-established wine-trade continued to flouish at Bordeaux, and salt from the Bay of Bourgneuf was a significant item. The English printing-presses depended largely on French paper, and linens from Normandy competed with those from the Low Countries. But intermittent war provided frequent interruptions, and it was impossible to pursue with France that continuous and expanding trade that was made possible by good diplomatic relations (and a common enemy) with the Netherlands.

Trade with Ireland continued throughout the century, though it was not of major importance. Ireland exported linen yarn in growing quantities, but her exports of manufactured linens and woollen mantles fell away, to the detriment of the native industries. Her greatest single export was fish, but this trade also declined in the later 16th century when the English ports (except for Bristol) were increasingly supplied direct from the Newfoundland banks. She could not offer a large market for English woollen cloth.

Thus, for a variety of reasons, some primarily economic, others mainly diplomatic or strategic, English trade in the early 16th century had come to be centred mainly on Antwerp. And just as dependence on a single industry had its dangers, so too had heavy reliance on a single market. In both cases the full dangers were not apparent till 1551. Until then expanding cloth exports went hand in hand with the booming prosperity of Antwerp. And the profits, while the going was good, went to the company of the Merchant Adventurers of London.

This company had grown up among English merchants trading to the Netherlands in the fourteenth and fifteenth centuries. These included outport merchants as well as Londoners, though the latter no doubt predominated from the start. Nor did the "company", amorphous and ill-defined as it was in the early years, consist only of cloth-exporters; the grants made to it by the governments of both countries may be read as including all Englishmen trading to the Netherlands. But by the end of the fifteenth century a distinct group had emerged, dominated by the Londoners and with a single Governor drawn from among the London merchants, possessed of its own coat of arms, and having successfully pre-empted the title "Adventurers" that had formerly applied to any merchant (other than a Stapler) trading overseas.

Parallel developments in London had drawn together merchants of the various great livery companies—Mercers, Drapers, Grocers, Haberdashers and others—who shared a common interest in the cloth-trade. The separate groups tended to coalesce round the Mercers, who formed the largest single group of cloth-exporters, and who supplied the nascent company with a meeting-place, a clerk, a minute-book and a treasure-chest. A common interest in organising regular cloth-shipments to the Netherlands bound these merchants ever closer together, while governments—both national and municipal—found it convenient to negotiate with them as a single body. Common interest and official pressure thus combined to weld the groups into a single unit, and this achieved formal recognition in 1486 when an act of the Common Council of London created a separate organisation for the Adventurers.

The official seat of government lay always in the

Netherlands, where elections were held, important legislation passed or ratified, and meetings of the General Court (the full assembly of the members) held. But since some two-thirds of merchants active in the Netherlands were Londoners, and since it would appear that the Governor was always a Londoner and probably at least eight of his twelve Assistants (the executive of the company) also Londoners, there is no reasonable doubt that the effective centre of authority lay in London. Even when in time the greater merchants ceased to visit the Netherlands in person, and were represented there by their apprentices or factors, they could easily maintain control. The provincial merchants, such as those of Newcastle, could do no more than vainly protest at the measures imposed by the dominant majority. Inside the London group the Mercers maintained their ascendancy for the first half of the century, though after 1526 the minutes of the Adventurers were separated from those of the Mercers and the Governor of the Company was no longer invariably drawn from among them. Mercers accounted for about 40 per cent of Londoners' cloth-exports up to 1547, and their dominance rested on economic strength as well as control of the official machinery. While it lasted, the vigour and health of England's export trade depended on the wisdom and probity of a single London livery company.

The Adventurers were a "regulated" company, that is to say they traded individually under an agreed set of regulations (like the Staplers of Calais); they did not pool their resources and trade as a body like the later joint-stock companies. Each merchant bought his own cloths on the best terms he could on the home market, sold them in person or through his factor at Antwerp, made his own decision as to whether to bring home the proceeds by bill of exchange or by purchasing goods for import, and in the latter case was responsible for the sale of his goods in London. The regulations related chiefly to the shipment of the cloths overseas and the broad conditions of sale abroad. For safety and convenience the Adventurers shipped their cloth jointly in periodic fleets, which in principle were sent to each of the four great annual marts at Antwerp and its satellite Bergen-op-Zoom. In practice it became usual to ship to only two or three marts a year, and to attend the others only to settle accounts or purchase goods for import. The allocation of space in the ships, freight charges and the conditions agreed with the ships' masters were all arranged by officials of the company. In time of war or threatened piracy armed convoys might be jointly hired by the members. In Antwerp or Bergen-op-Zoom, the merchants had to display their cloths together and on stipulated days. This was presumably to limit competition and prevent undercutting, though there seems to be no evidence of agreements to fix prices. Beyond these general regulations, and some restrictions on the conduct and choice of residence of the younger merchants, the Adventurers were left freedom of action. Their fellowship gave them relative security against the hazards of the seas and the arbitrariness of foreign officials; it could not make their profits for them nor prevent their going bankrupt.

Many criticisms have been levelled at the Adventurers, both at the time of their greatness and since. It can fairly be alleged that they belied their name. So far from adventuring, at least in the modern sense of the word, they pursued a safety-first policy of easy profits in an assured market. They did not make voyages of discovery or develop new markets. The sea-voyage from London to Antwerp was the shortest trade-route that could well be imagined. They did not encourage any diversity in the export trade; they simply expanded sales of woollen cloth. They did not innovate in the sphere of company organisation; their general structure and many of their specific regulations were clearly copied from the Staplers of Calais. They were slow to adopt new devices of commercial technique; neither double-entry book-keeping nor marine insurance made much headway in England in the first half of the century. But was there any good reason —from their point of view—to do any of these things?

They had no incentive to forsake a tried market for the uncertainties of new ones. At Antwerp they could depend on finding eager customers for their cloth. They had expended much money and energy in obtaining privileges and concessions from both national and municipal governments in the Netherlands, so that at Antwerp, Bergen and Middelburg they enjoyed judicial immunities and tax reliefs that made them the most favoured foreign nation trading in the country. Indeed they held in the Netherlands a position corresponding to that of the Hansards in England—they were better-off than the native inhabitants, and incurred similar jealousies and resentments. Their shipments were continuous and secure; neither war nor piracy, embargo nor sequestration, prevented the London merchant Thomas Kitson from sending at least one shipment of cloth to the Netherlands every year from 1512 to 1539. The cloth trade, in spite of some severe short-term fluctuations, expanded continuously up to 1551, from just over 50,000 annually in the first few years of Henry VII's reign to over 120,000 cloths in Henry VIII's last years. The profits of individuals could run high. Kitson sold his clothes at a gross profit of between 20 and 25 per cent in 1521–23; the accounts of Thomas Gresham for the years 1546–51 suggest net profits on his whole business of nearly 15 per cent, which meant that he could expect to double his capital every five years. What temptation was there for such fortunate men to experiment or seek change?

It might also be suggested that the Company was oligarchic in its structure, profit and power being monopolised by a few rich men. It is certainly true that only a handful of merchants were responsible for the bulk of the cloth-exports. In a group of 131 Adventurers who shipped to the great summer mart at Antwerp in 1535 a mere seventeen owned nearly half the cloths. It is also true that there was a slight but clear tendency for fewer and fewer merchants to handle more and more of the woollens during the early 16th century. The higher offices in the Company tended to be occupied by the wealthier London merchants, though the Governorship often went to a diplomatist rather than a trader. But such a situation was quite normal in this period, when city governments, like that of Exeter, were usually controlled by a minority of the rich, and when gilds and livery companies everywhere were becoming more oligarchic. The Mercers at least were able to check the arrogance of their leading members, as when in 1483 Governor John Pickering appeared before the Wardens "all haughty and royal", refused to take off his cap, and boastfully advanced his own great services to the company; he had to beg the company's pardon on bended knee; clearly the corporate dignity of the fellowship set bounds on the pretensions of its individual members. Above all, it must be stressed that the turn-over in the Adventurers' membership was very rapid—at least 80 per cent every twenty years. Any inner ring that established itself was thus necessarily only temporary; there was no ruling caste that handed on power from generation to generation. Oligarchy was tempered by mortality.

The Adventurers were also accused of being exclusive and restrictive. After a struggle with the Staplers the Adventurers succeeded in 1516 in compelling them to join their own company if they wished to take part in the Netherlands cloth-trade. But this dispute was largely shadow-boxing, since many Staplers were already Adventurers, and the decline of their company meant that in any case they could not long compete with their more powerful rivals. More serious were the periodic attempts to restrict membership, especially that of the outport merchants. These were rarely the sons or apprentices of Adventurers, and being thus debarred from admission to the company by patrimony or apprenticeship could join only by "redemption"—that is, paying an admission fee. An attempt was made in the 1490's to raise this to the prohibitive level of £20, but an act of 1497 reduced this to the more tolerable level of ten marks (£6 – 13 – 4). In 1523 there was talk of petitioning parliament to raise this to £40, but nothing came of the suggestion. Thus though the intention of the London oligarchs was

3

only too clear, they did not in fact succeed in squeezing out their provincial competitors. The latter could join in the lucrative cloth-trade to the Netherlands and enjoy the protection of the company's organisation provided only they could raise the sum of ten marks. Even this might seem considerable to the lesser outport merchants, but their complaints were not altogether reasonable. It cost money to obtain and keep up the amenities offered by the company, and clearly these had to be paid for. The recalcitrant merchants of Newcastle were like poor men seeking to join a comfortable club without paying for the privilege.

Nor, at least until 1551, is there any evidence that the Adventurers conspired to hold down the price of cloth at home or restrict export abroad. The account-books of Kitson and Gresham suggest on the contrary that they eagerly competed for limited supplies of cloth on the home market, offering down-payments to secure a clothier's output in advance. In such a seller's market it was obviously not possible for them to depress prices artificially. Equally, a single merchant might export nearly 2,000 cloths in a year, as did Thomas Lodge in 1547–48, and there was clearly no attempt to impose a "stint of trade". This was a later invention.

With all this said, it remains true that the Adventurers' trading policy in the first half of the century, however intelligible from their viewpoint, had grave dangers for themselves and for the nation. Their highly concentrated activities were very vulnerable to any crisis in their single market, and the discomfiture of the Adventurers would bring about that of the clothiers who supplied them with their wares. Just such a crisis developed at the mid-point of the century, reaching a climax in 1551. It was this that abruptly ended the steady expansion of the cloth-trade, disappointed the comfortable expectations of Thomas Gresham, and forced English trade into new markets and new forms of commercial organisation. It marked the end of a distinctive period in English commerce, and the beginning of a new era.

The last years of Henry VIII's reign saw a rapid boom

in cloth-exports. Those for London alone averaged 99,000 in 1542–44, rose to 119,000 in 1545–47, and reached as high as 133,000 in 1550. This boom was partly artificial in character. Debasement of the coinage in England, beginning in 1543, produced rapid price-inflation that at first stimulated trade. English cloth was for a time relatively cheap for the foreign purchaser, since prices moved more slowly than the rate of exchange on the Antwerp Bourse. But this could not go on indefinitely, and in 1550 the Antwerp market reached saturation-point, the Adventurers could no longer sell their cloth, and the cloth industry was already approaching stagnation by the spring of 1550. There followed an orgy of mutual recrimination, in which the older and richer merchants blamed their younger and less responsible fellows, both groups blamed the clothiers for producing shoddy goods that would not sell, and the clothiers themselves divided into those who blamed the merchants for deliberately holding down prices and those who blamed their young competitors for bad workmanship. There is indeed some evidence of bad workmanship, and English merchants at this time had frequently to allow rebates to their customers for cloths that were short of their advertised length or else badly made. There is very little to be said for the other accusations, which seem to have been part of a general hunt for scapegoats. The crisis was in the main simply a crisis of over-production, both merchants and clothiers having snatched incautiously at opportunities that briefly presented themselves. A reaction was bound to follow.

Other factors aggravated the crisis. With successive debasements of the currency the exchange-rate as between London and Antwerp moved rapidly to the disadvantage of sterling, and the pound reached a nadir in July 1551 when it was quoted at 13s. 4gr. in Flemish currency. This damaged the credit of English merchants in the Netherlands, while at the same time the hoarding of specie in England made it difficult for them to export currency to meet debts at Antwerp or Calais. Clumsy and ill-timed efforts by the government to bring about a deflation in the summer of 1551 produced complete financial confusion in England. When the deflation did take effect it had the result of raising the price of cloth in the Netherlands, and hopes of a recovery in that market were thus killed. An attempt by some of the merchants to find an alternative outlet at Bordeaux proved abortive, as too many had the same idea, with the result that by September there was a glut of cloth there also. The city, remarked one of them, was thronged with "such a sort of merchants as I think came not out of England many a day".

Minor contributory factors were religious persecution and plague. In 1550 Charles V launched a new campaign against heresy in the Netherlands, and in July the Privy Council warned the Adventurers to withdraw their goods from Antwerp. Henceforth the English "heretics", along with German Lutherans and Portuguese Jews, could no longer feel secure in that city. In March 1551 came a serious outbreak of a mysterious sweating sickness, especially severe in the towns, which before it ended in July of the same year had struck hard at the London merchant community. How many died of it can only be guessed, but contemporary letters suggest that few families escaped altogether. Clearly this plague cannot be reckoned a cause of the commercial crisis, but the death of many leading merchants and their factors certainly lessened the chance of a quick recovery.

Whatever the relative importance of the different factors involved, and however contemporaries disagreed in their analysis of the event, no-one doubted the seriousness of the crisis. A seemingly safe market had collapsed with disastrous effect, and the dangers of putting all one's commercial eggs into one basket were glaringly apparent. There could be no sure expectation that the cloth-trade would recover and continue its former expansion, as it had done after earlier, less serious depressions. Merely withholding one shipment of cloth till the market recovered would not serve this time. New markets had to be developed both to absorb English cloth-exports and to spread the risks more widely.

This is not to say that all attempts at exploration and colonisation in the later 16th century were inspired by a search for new markets. It is true that Richard Hakluyt, in the dedication of the second edition of *The Principal Navigations* (1599), writes to Robert Cecil that "our chief desire is to find out ample vent of our woollen cloth, the natural commodity of this our Realm", but not all explorers shared Hakluyt's special preoccupation, and many of them were looking quite simply for the easy riches that had rewarded the first Spanish invaders of the New World. But certainly the merchants seized their opportunities, and Hakluyt was at least being wise after the event. The second half of the century did see the re-establishment of English trade in areas that it had largely forsaken, and its extension into new ones not previously known.

In the Mediterranean a revival began with the development of trade with Morocco. The first origins of this are a little obscure, but the traditional date of 1551 for the first voyage there is probably correct. Morocco offered a possible, if limited market for English cloth, and in return could supply the sugar for which demand at home was increasing. Though some other goods went out to Morocco—linen and canvas and even some arms—and though some other imports—almonds, aniseed and even gold—came thence, the trade consisted essentially in the exchange of cloth for sugar. In 1574–75 sugar accounted for about 85 per cent of goods brought home, and though the proportion later dropped to about 70 per cent the preponderance of this one commodity remained firm.

The trade was conducted by individual merchants who sometimes formed partnerships and usually worked through factors. There was no regulation of their activities before 1585, though from time to time the formation of a chartered company was proposed. The usual arguments were brought forward—that it was necessary to stop the trafficking in undesirable goods and to prevent a horde of irresponsible young men from spoiling the market for their seniors. When a company, usually known for convenience as the Barbary Company, was formed in 1585, the pressure came mainly from the Earl of Leicester and his merchant associates; its vague informal clauses, probably modelled on the Levant Company's charter of 1581, gave the Earl a dominant say in the company's affairs. It lasted twelve years, and probably made very little difference to the conduct of the trade. Being a regulated, not a joint-stock, company its members traded individually as before. Trade was apparently not strictly limited to the charter members, no stint of trade was set, no staple town in Morocco appointed. It came to an end in 1597 without any protest, which suggests that it had served little practical purpose and that the merchants felt they could well do without it.

The history of Leicester's own partnership inside the framework of the Barbary Company illustrates the difficulties of the Moroccan trade. After four years of trading the original capital of £5000 had gone, partly because of the sum of £4000 paid to the King of Morocco for a licence and partly because of the inordinate salaries and expenses allowed to the factors and servants of the company. It is also interesting that Leicester's company consistently failed to make any profit on its imports to England, even on sugar, and presumably persisted in them only because it was impossible to return the proceeds of cloth-sales by bill of exchange. Other merchants may not have been so improvident as the Leicester partnership, but they too suffered from the general difficulties of dealing in a country where their tenure was precarious, and where both the King and the Jewish middle-men with whom they dealt were liable to prove bad debtors. It is hardly surprising that the trade was only a small one, and that in 1598–99 exports to Morocco amounted to a mere £7400.

Contact with the eastern Mediterranean was renewed a little later than with the western. From about 1570 onwards the English were brought to that area, like the Dutch and the Hansards, by the rising demand for northern grain and fish from a population that was pressing on the limits of subsistence. The English could in addition supply the lead and tin needed for arms, and were thus sure of a welcome. Danger of Turkish attacks was reduced after the battle of Lepanto in 1571, though the corsairs of Algiers and Tripoli remained a scourge of the entire sea for decades to come. The northern powers were able, too, to take advantage of Venice's weakness after her truce with the Ottomans in 1573, a date which marks the end of the Republic's short-lived recovery in the Mediterranean spice-trade.

Negotiations with the Sultan led to a grant of 35 capitulations in June 1580, which assured the English merchants of reasonable safety in the Levant. This was followed by the incorporation in September 1581 of the Levant Company, a joint-stock company that shared some members in common with the Barbary Company, and whose moving spirits were the rich London merchants Edward Osborne and Richard Staper. This company prospered from the start, realising profits of 300 per cent in its early years, and going from strength to strength in the 1590's, after absorbing the short-lived Venice Company. Already by 1595 the company disposed of 15 ships, and by 1599 had 20 in Italian waters alone. By the end of the century an efficient convoy system had been established to ward off the attacks of the corsairs, and the English, while concentrating especially on Syria, were active throughout the entire Mediterranean. Their more regular trading activities were centred at Leghorn in the western Mediterranean, where the Medici Grand Dukes of Tuscany were attempting to rebuild the commercial fortunes of Florence, and in Smyrna and Aleppo to the east. Less orthodox traders, operating outside the Levant Company, did a lively business in arms and slaves for Venetians and Turks impartially, while legitimate attacks on Spanish shipping were followed by indiscriminate piracy at the expense of French and Italian merchants also. In short, the English were to be found wherever profits were to be made.

The second half of the century saw also a revival of

English trade in the Baltic. The political strength of the Hanseatic League had long been on the decline, divided as it was into three increasingly distinct groups of cities. The leadership of Lübeck was weakened and discredited by a crushing naval defeat at the hands of Sweden and Denmark in 1535, and her participation in the struggle between Denmark and Sweden in 1563–70 brought more loss than gain. The economic decline of the League was slower and less obvious, but Dutch and even South German competition in the Baltic was increasing by the mid-century, and the suspension of Hansard privileges in England in 1552, though only temporary, was a symptom of growing general weakness. By the 1560's the Hansards had lost their control of the export of English cloth to north-east Germany, and from this time on English merchants, from both London and the east-coast ports, handled the bulk of the trade. Officially this was concentrated in the hands of the Eastland Company (1579). This did not create a new outlet for English cloth, but rather organised and canalised the efforts of merchants already active in the Baltic, affording them some protection against piracy and a united front against Hanse resistance. Since Danzig continued to be unfriendly to the English the main staple of the new regulated company was located at Elbing, a German city on Polish territory. The English did much to restore the fortunes of that decayed port, unsatisfactory as its facilities were, and in 1594 English cloth made up six-sevenths of the Elbing's imports. But it was not a satisfactory substitute for Danzig, and the Company was unable to prevent its members from trading there altogether. Danzig remained the main market for Baltic grain, and in the early 17th century the Eastland Company finally settled there.

By the end of the century Hansard competition was much weaker. The League's privileges in England were drastically cut down in 1578–79, and in 1598 the famous Steelyard was closed. This decline was mainly due to the divisions within the League and to the growing dominance of Dutch shipping in the Baltic. By 1600 more than 80 per cent of the ships passing through the Danish Sound were Dutch. Too much credit should not be given to the English merchants for the discomfiture of their old rivals; they profited from a situation made for them by the efforts and mistakes of others. It was nonetheless a considerable success for the English merchants that they were able to re-enter the Baltic, and that at least the English cloth trade there was conducted by them and not the Hansards. The real turning-point came in the 1560's. The year 1598 had only symbolic importance.

The Russia Company (1555) followed the celebrated attempt of Willoughby and Chancellor in 1553 to discover a north-east passage to the Indies. The purpose of the promoters of this voyage was at least in part to find a new market for cloth, for, as they declared later, it had been found "inconvenient that the utterance of the commodities of England, especially cloth, should so depend upon the Low Countries and Spain." The explorers did not find their way to the Indies, nor did they discover the spices and treasure which were also prime objectives of the original expedition. But two years later a new company was incorporated with 201 members, and valuable privileges that included a monopoly of the northern route to Russia, freedom from customs, and the right to trade throughout Russia, were obtained from Ivan IV, who hoped in return for diplomatic advantage and the help of western technicians. The Tsar gained less than he had hoped, and the merchants failed to maintain a monopoly of the northern route or to sell as much cloth as they wished. Nonetheless, the year 1555 marks the beginning of an appreciable trade with Russia, and perhaps the first opening of a "window to the west."

The Russia Company was from the first a joint-stock company, and though its early financial history is obscure and involved it seems to have been regarded as offering a fairly safe and permanent investment. This form of organisation had much to recommend it when a new and uncertain market was being opened up, when shipping was limited to certain months in the year, and when it was necessary to

3*

maintain permanent representatives in Russia to negotiate purchases during the winter months. These special problems of the Russia trade made it desirable to concentrate the trade in the hands of the Company's factors, whose hand was strengthened in bargaining by representing the whole body of merchants, and who could plan in advance to avoid the risk of ships returning home half-empty. But even joint-stock organisation could not obviate the typical problem of the interloper trading within the company's area, and the fact that the Russia Company was by the 1620's a regulated company like the Merchant Adventurers shows that the joint-stock form was not indispensable to the trade when once established.

The trade was not substantial by comparison with some older-established branches. In 1587, the peak year of Elizabeth's reign, ten ships brought cargoes of tallow, wax, cordage, flax and hides worth perhaps £25,000 from St. Nicholas. Exports to Russia were untypical in that they were more varied than those to other markets, consisting in part of re-exported wines and foodstuffs, while the cloth that was the largest single item among them was exported dyed and finished. The cloth did not sell very well in Russia, perhaps because of its high price, and other goods also sold slowly. The fact that in 1582 and 1584 the Company obtained licences to export bullion suggests that the balance of trade was unfavourable. Attempts to develop a trade-route through Russia to Persia proved unsuccessful. They failed to realise profits for their promoters and the founding of the Levant Company made the route less necessary. The reluctance of the Tsar to permit free passage through his lands was a secondary cause of failure. Measured in strictly quantitative terms the Russia Company was only a partial success.

Such measurement is, however, unfair to it. The value of the ship-building materials brought home cannot be assessed in money terms only at a time when they were urgently needed for strategic purposes. Nor can the importance of a trade with a long future be measured solely by its modest beginnings. Both as pioneers in a new market and the founders of the first major joint-stock company in England the Muscovy Merchants of 1555 deserve all the credit that historians have given them.

The same arguments apply *a fortiori* to the East India trade. The impetus towards its founding came in part from the desire of the Levant merchants to extend their range and obtain their spices at source, in part from the difficulties of European trade at the time of the Armada, and in part from the spectacularly successful example of the Dutch. A first expedition under James Lancaster in 1591 did not prove a success, but Dutch expeditions in 1598 and 1599 prompted the English merchants to renewed efforts. A charter was obtained for a new company in December 1600, and four of its ships, again under Lancaster, sailed in the following year. Although backed by over a hundred London merchants, who had promised to subscribe £30,000, the efforts of the company did not remotely match those of the Dutch in the early years. They suffered from a relative shortage of capital and shipping, from a less purposeful and coherent organisation, and from less enthusiastic support from their government. But a great enterprise was under way before the last Tudor died, and when we think of the later triumphs of the East India Company we should remember gratefully the exertions of Edward Osborne and Richard Staper, the Levant merchants who set it in motion.

A form of commercial enterprise that became especially popular in the last decades of the 16th century was investment in privateering expeditions. This, of course, became a patriotic duty when war with Spain had broken out, and had some strategic importance in diverting Spanish naval resources away from European waters. It was also a profitable activity for wealthy London merchants like John Watts, John More and Thomas Myddelton, who could afford to invest in a whole series of expeditions and spread their risks accordingly. Cargoes of spices and dyes (more rarely silver) intercepted in the West Indies could bring the investor a spectacular return. It is difficult to estimate the normal profits of such investment, and perhaps misleading to talk of "average" profits in enterprises which might end in vast gain (Watts may have made £40,000 in 1591) or total loss—including loss of life. The regular investor might make profits of 50 per cent over a period; the small man might make a fortune or be ruined.

Nor is it easy to say whether the country as a whole profited from piracy in the long run. Some commodities—silks, spices and dyes—became more widely and cheaply available; some native industries, such as sugar-refining, may have been stimulated. Privateering also made a contribution to the war against Spain and served as a training for English navigators and seamen. On the other hand money and energy was diverted from more solid and reputable forms of activity for the sake of quick profits in an industry that could have no permanent future. It is, of course, impossible to say how in fact English trade would have prospered in the 1580's and 1590's without the distraction of privateering, and the war itself was clearly a disruptive force. The East India Company and early colonising ventures were often financed in part by merchants who had made good in piracy, but the Roanoke settlement of 1585 was not a success and Lancaster's eastern voyage of 1591 was not followed up for eight years. The balance of profit is impossible to determine.

While English exports began to move to new markets in the later 16th century, their composition also became more diverse. The broadcloth continued to dominate, but lighter cloths, more suitable for the Levant and other warm climates, made their appearance on an increasing scale. These "new draperies" were especially prominent in Norwich and the surrounding area, where Flemish and Walloon immigrants, fleeing from religious persecution at home, introduced and established them. The production of bays, says, grograms and other cheap, light cloths proceeded apace from the 1560's onwards. The contribution of the alien settlers can be seen in the records of the Norwich Cloth Halls—an increase from about 3,400 a year in 1566–70 to 36,300 in the years 1584–88. It was not until the middle of James I's reign that broadcloths ceased to dominate the export trade. But at least by the end of Elizabeth's reign that trade was not so overwhelmingly dependent on a single branch of the woollen textile industry.

Was there an expansion of English overseas trade in Elizabeth's reign? In a geographical sense there undoubtedly was, and in 1603 the activities of the Levant Company, the Russia Company and the East India Company showed how far English commerce had extended its range. But the importance of these new markets must not be exaggerated. An analysis of London customs accounts from September 1587 to April 1588 shows some 70 per cent of the entries to come from ports concentrated on the North European coast from Hamburg to Rouen, with the heaviest concentration at Stade and Middelburg, the staples of the Merchant Adventurers. It is true that an analysis of customs entries may misrepresent the scope of the trade; from the same analysis it appears that 31 entries from St. Nicholas represented goods of more value than those listed in 307 entries from Rouen. But there is little doubt that the bulk of England's trade, though no longer centred on a single port, still found its outlet in the traditional market of the Adventurers. St. Nicholas, Aleppo and Bantam were only minor outposts in England's commercial empire.

The new companies also saw an extension of the trading community outside the ranks of merchants. In the old regulated companies, of course, only active traders could be members, and there was little scope for the sleeping partner or passive investor. In the joint-stock companies it was possible for non-merchants to participate, since no special knowledge or exertion was required—only willingness to risk one's money. The Russia Company at its foundation included seven peers, eight important office-holders, fourteen knights (of whom four were aldermen), seven aldermen, eleven esquires and eight gentlemen. No doubt some of these, especially the aldermen, had commercial or industrial interests already, but most of this group would not be found in either the Merchant Adventurers' or the Staplers' companies. The Russia Company was admittedly exceptional in this respect, and other companies had only a small sprinkling of non-merchants—such as Leicester and Warwick in the Barbary Company. It is difficult to say, too, how many of these gentry were active members of these companies even in the financial sense. Naturally the main conduct of trade remained always in the hands of *bona fide* merchants. But it had at least been shown that trading capital could be raised outside the merchant community, and not only for the privateering expeditions that were similarly backed by courtiers and gentry.

In other respects it is difficult to argue that there was any great expansion of trade in Elizabeth's reign. There are no full and reliable figures to show its total volume, and those available for London's cloth-exports suggest a relative stability from 1574 onwards, but at a level below the mid-century peak. There were severe depressions in the early 1560's and the early 1570's, and a sharp crisis in 1586–87. Figures for customs receipts suggest considerable fluctuations in the 1590's. But cloth-exports are not so satisfactory an index of national trade in 1600 as in 1540, and customs receipts may vary with the efficiency of officials as well as with the trade itself. Smuggling and customs-evasion undoubtedly increased greatly after the revision of duties in 1558 that made such activities more profitable and the risks worth taking. Not all trade is recorded in the customers' books. In the present state of the evidence it is impossible to be dogmatic. It seems likely that the failure of the cloth-trade to continue its expansion may have been off-set by the development of other exports and re-exports, and that the increasing comfort of at least the wealthier classes in Elizabethan society reflects a growing import-trade. A large increase in volume, however, would be hard to prove.

The second half of the century was also marked by restrictive practices. These had not been wholly absent in the first half, but the attempts of the Merchant Adventurers to confine their lucrative trade to a narrow ring of London merchants had been restrained both by government intervention and the absence of any compelling need to limit an expanding trade. The crisis of 1550–51 saw a revival of exclusivism. One return of it was the temporary suspension of Hanse privileges in 1552. Another was the raising of the Adventurers' entrance fee from ten to a hundred marks in 1555, thus in effect shutting out the provincial merchants. Another was the more monopolistic charter obtained by the Adventurers in 1564, and yet another their introduction at some unknown date of a "stint of trade" that limited individual merchants to exporting only a specified number of cloths per year, a number that varied with the seniority of the merchant. Other companies had their allotted monopoly area, and in principle confined trade in it to members of the company. The idea was to share out what trade there was—and contemporaries tended to think of it as limited and fixed—among a small number of men. Likewise the merchants may have looked back on the series of minor crises that led up to 1550—there was one at the start of nearly every decade—and sought to prevent their recurrence or mitigate their effects by stricter control. In practice the would-be monopolists were often thwarted by interlopers who traded in their area without joining the company who nominally controlled it. The Adventurers could not prevent interlopers from trading at Hamburg, and even the Russia Company was unable to maintain a strict monopoly. But the intention to restrict trade was clearly marked, and is not consistent with the idea that the Elizabethans were, as a group, enterprising and adventurous men.

Nor was very much enterprise shown by Tudor merchants in commercial methods and organisation. The joint-stock company was indeed an innovation, but it did not survive very long in either the Russian or the Levant trade. Increas-

ing use was made of the resident factor or agent abroad, this
being essential for the joint-stock company and highly desirable for the individual wealthy merchant with numerous
irons in the fire. The factor might be a fully-qualified merchant, perhaps lacking capital to set up in business on his
own, who acted for one or more principals in a foreign port,
sometimes on a commission basis. Such was the position of
Thomas Malliard, factor for Thomas Howell at Seville in
1521, and of Blase and Thomas Freman, factors to Thomas
Sexton in Danzig in the 1550's. Or he might be a young man
still in or barely out of his apprenticeship, acting for his
master. It was in this capacity that Thomas Washington
worked for Thomas Kitson at Antwerp in 1536; an account
of his transactions at the midsummer mart has survived. In
1589 there appeared a manual for the instruction of such
young men, *The marchants avizo* by John Browne of Bristol,
which combined much sound practical information with a
good deal of pious persuasion. The growing practice of dele-
gating business and responsibility to such agents made it
possible for the 16th century merchant both to enlarge the
scope of his affairs and also to be increasingly stay-at-home.
But no English business house of this period attained the
scope and complexity of the contemporary Augsburg bank-
ing houses like the Fugger and Welser, nor even of the 15th
century Medici. The use of factors allowed the Elizabethan
merchant to be sedentary; it did not make him an international tycoon.

English merchants were similarly slow to follow foreign
example in matters of commercial technique. True, they
made increasing use of bills of exchange, and the form of these
was gradually assimilated to the more succinct and business-
like Italian model. It was a commonplace of the period that
merchants could no more do without such bills than a ship
without water. But marine insurance was slow to develop.
Its laws and practices were uncertain, its status at law
dubious, and aggrieved parties found it hard to obtain legal
remedy. A monopoly for the registration of insurance policies,

granted in 1576, aroused general dissatisfaction, and a statute of 1601 that attempted to give Chancery jurisdiction in cases of insurance failed to clear up the legal tangle. In fact insurance was probably not much used, especially in the earlier part of the century. For the short cross-Channel shipments of the Adventurers it was sufficient to split the risk by dividing one's cloths among a number of ships. Not until longer voyages with correspondingly higher risks became common was there urgent need to resort to marine insurance. It is not surprising that up to the end of the 16th century its practice remained in an immature and confused state. Bookkeeping also remained backward by the best European standards. Double-entry book-keeping had been known in Italy for some two centuries, but surviving Tudor specimens of it show poor technique and a failure to understand the purposes and advantages of the system. Again, it had little to offer the 16th century merchant. For his relatively simple business a single-entry system was quite adequate to keep track of his doings, and periodic inventories of his stock and debts served the purpose of the modern balance-sheet. Only a few large and complex concerns could profit from the instruction offered in the text-books on double-entry accounting that appeared in England from 1543. The ledgers of lesser firms were no doubt, in the words of one author anxious to sell his treatise, "so grossly, obscurely and lewdly kept, that after their decease neither wife, servant, executor nor other could by their books perceive what of right appertained to them to be received of other, neither what justly was due by them unto other." But the English book-keepers knew quite enough for their purposes.

The death of Elizabeth I found London still dominating the whole field of overseas trade, if not perhaps to the extent the customs accounts would have us believe. Woollen cloth, and especially west country broadcloths, still accounted for the bulk of the country's exports. Most of these still found their outlet immediately across the Channel. English merchants, even the greatest of them, still lagged behind their more outstanding foreign rivals in their wealth, the size and complexity of their business, and in their grasp of commercial technique. In these respects the situation of 1485 remained substantially unchanged. But new markets had been found, new companies incorporated to exploit them, new varieties of cloth produced to sell in them. English merchants handled the bulk of the export-trade. The east-coast ports could look forward to an expansion of their trade with the Baltic and the growth of the coal-trade. In the west Bristol was already profiting from the Newfoundland fisheries, and a century later would benefit from the colonies in the New World. The restrictive monopolies of the great London companies were faced with a vigorous challenge both from private interlopers and parliamentary critics. If the material achievements of Tudor commerce were a little unimpressive, there was plenty of promise for the future. Pioneers there had been, and the Stuart merchants would reap the fruits of their enterprise.

III

INDUSTRY AND THE TOWNS

SINCE WOOLLEN CLOTH continued to be England's major export throughout the 16th century, it is hardly surprising that the woollen industry was much the most important in the Tudor period. Contemporaries, statesmen and publicists alike, were agreed in stressing its vital contribution to the country's prosperity. Travellers like Leland had eyes only for the clothing towns when they made their perambulations of the realm; other industries received only the scantiest attention. This consensus of opinion is so strong that it is easy for us to suppose that no other significant manufactures existed, and that "industrial labourer" is synonymous with

"clothworker". Such a conclusion would be very misleading.

In the first place many skilled artisans worked at crafts
that did not produce for the foreign market. A study of
occupational groupings in Coventry, Northampton and
Leicester in the early 16th century suggests that the
clothing trade (for the domestic market) employed some
15 per cent of the population; the food and drink trades
gave work to a further 12 to 21 per cent; the building trade
occupied some 4 to 7½ per cent. If these figures are typical of
Tudor provincial towns in general, then about 35 to 40 per
cent of the urban workers in them were engaged in these
three major occupations. In Coventry the textile industry
gave work to a third of the workers, as might have been expected, but at Northampton and Leicester only 13½ per cent
and 8½ per cent were thus engaged. In all three towns the
leather industry was of considerable importance, the figures
ranging from 11 per cent in Coventry to as much as 23 per
cent in Northampton. It seems likely, indeed, that this industry has been unduly neglected by historians, who have
been excessively preoccupied either with the established
cloth trade or the nascent mining and metallurgical industries. In Northampton the leather workers were the
largest single group, and clearly the importance of this craft
cannot be measured by its insignificant record in the customs
books. It admittedly showed no spectacular developments
in the course of the century, but it afforded a livelihood
to many humble townspeople. Its contemporary importance
was to some extent recognised by the frequency of legislation
to regulate it.

Building was another industry that employed substantial
numbers, and the masons' lodges were already established
all over the country. Though the labour force was by its
nature mobile and dispersed its organisation was effective
enough to secure a good level of wages for its members.
Every town of any size had its brewers, and the 16th century
saw a change of taste from ale to beer. Once again, there was

a steady demand on the home market, even if exports were confined mainly to supplying English soldiers or merchants overseas.

The much-publicised cloth industry saw no very striking developments, apart from the growth of the "new draperies" at the end of the century. Nor was the rapid expansion of the early Tudor period continued in the second half of the century, though lack of information about home consumption makes it dangerous to be dogmatic. The coal industry showed a much more impressive growth, while the metallurgical crafts showed more striking technical innovations. At least one historian has been so deeply impressed by these as to attribute an "industrial revolution" to the period 1540–1640. This is probably going too far, but Professor Nef has nonetheless done us useful service in emphasising the importance of industries other than woollen textiles.

With these reservations it remains true that the cloth industry deserves pride of place, and that for most of the century broadcloths and kerseys were England's foremost industrial product. Their manufacture was concentrated in three main areas. The most important of these was the western group of counties—Somerset, Gloucestershire, and most especially Wiltshire—whence came the "Worcesters" and "Castlecombes" that feature in Tudor merchants' account-books. This was the area of the broadcloth, though kerseys were produced to the east of the area, in parts of Berkshire and Oxfordshire. Newbury was an outstanding centre of kersey manufacture in the early 16th century, thanks mainly to the Winchcombe family. The wealthiest member of this family, John Winchcombe or "Jack of Newbury" was the hero of a well-known ballad by Thomas Deloney, and Winchcombe kerseys had an international reputation. East Anglia was a second flourishing area of cloth-manufacture, and its greatest clothiers, such as the Springs of Lavenham, rivalled any west country producer. By contrast with the unfinished broadcloths of Wiltshire—the "whites" of contemporary accounts —those of East Anglia were often dyed and finished before being exported. The same is true of the small but high-quality cloth-manufacture of Kent, which specialised in a russet cloth that cost between £5 and £7 in the early 1530's. The level of technical skill both in weaving and finishing must have been high to justify such prices—west country "whites" averaged only about £3 at this date. The third main area of production was Yorkshire, which manufactured mainly the cheaper and coarser kerseys and "dozens", often used by the merchants as wrappers for the more expensive cloths that they exported. Production was on a considerable scale, but did not rival either that of the west country or East Anglia in quality and price.

Some other counties also made cloth. Devonshire kerseys feature occasionally among the exports of the Merchant Adventurers. So too do the "cottons" (actually coarse woollen cloths) of Cheshire and Lancashire. Welsh woollens found a ready market in northern France, and the prosperity of Shrewsbury was largely due to its possession of the staple for Welsh cloth. But these areas could not be considered as cloth-producing areas comparable to Wiltshire, Somerset, Yorkshire and Suffolk, and though cloth-manufacture was widespread it was heavily concentrated in a few favoured counties.

A number of factors combined to determine the location of the industry. A ready supply of raw material was an obvious essential, and the west country cloth industry was largely based on Cotswold wool. But wool could be transported with relative ease, and in point of fact the clothing counties were not identical with the wool-producing ones. Probably more important was a supply of running water, since this was necessary to work the fulling-mills that performed an essential part of the process of manufacture. It was mainly for this reason that the English woollen industry was so dispersed and agrarian in character, by contrast with the urbanised industry of 13th century Flanders. Whereas the cloth-production of medieval Flanders was concentrated in the great cities of Ghent, Ypres and Bruges, that of 16th century Wiltshire straggled along the valleys of the Avon and Wylye; its centres were not great cities, but small towns and villages—Devizes, Warminster, Westbury and Lacock. Lavenham was only a small Suffolk town even by the modest standards of the age. A third set of factors has recently been suggested, stressing social conditions rather than geographical or economic ones. Rural industry is often to be found where the density of population is high, and where the division of the family inheritance among the surviving sons multiplies holdings. This seems to be especially true of areas where holdings are relatively secure—either freehold or copyhold. Where such a population is mainly occupied in pastoral and dairy farming, which make comparatively light demands on labour, there is both the need and the opportunity to supplement a meagre farming income by part-time industry. This explanation has not yet been worked out in detail for the whole of England, but seems to fit the facts in some areas very well. It would certainly help to explain the presence of a well-developed cloth-industry in Wiltshire, Suffolk and Yorkshire; conversely it would explain the absence of it in an arable county like Hertfordshire, where the population was fully occupied in tillage. Population pressure, in short, may well have been a major determinant in the siting of early industries.

The importance of cloth in England's export trade made the health of the industry dangerously dependent on the state of the foreign market, all the more dangerously when that market was so small and concentrated in the first half of the century. A temporary suspension of shipments to Antwerp could cause considerable under-employment and hardship in the clothing counties, though during the first half of the century such interruptions did not usually last long. The trade crisis of 1550–51 was much more severe, and produced in more prolonged and extreme terms all the usual arguments—from the clothiers that the merchants refused to buy their wares, and from the merchants that they could not afford to buy them while shipments to the Netherlands were suspended. In such conditions the wealthy clothiers had no hesitation in laying off large numbers of spinners and weavers, and the impact of a trade crisis thus fell quite quickly on those least able to bear it. Acute hardship would be felt in areas, such as Wiltshire, where many families were wholly dependent on the cloth trade for their livelihood. Outside such areas, at least in the earlier part of the century, unemployed clothworkers might be able to find work on the land. It was normal for families to combine pastoral farming with work in the cloth industry—if only to the extent that the womenfolk were engaged in spinning—and a trade crisis therefore meant underemployment rather than unemployment for the family. When so many lived at mere subsistence level this was serious enough, but not as catastrophic as it would be in an age of greater specialisation. Specialisation probably did increase during the century as population grew, and more workers came to be dependent on industrial wages alone. But by the end of the century both the cloth industry and its markets were more diversified, and the collapse of a single market not so serious. A general depression, on the other hand, would cause more widespread distress than ever before.

The cloth industry was organised in what is often known as the "domestic system". This implies that the humbler clothworkers normally worked in their own homes and workshops and had their raw materials supplied to them by the clothiers, who later took back the cloth either to pass it on for completion of the next process of manufacture or to sell it in London or some other market. Workers would be paid at piece-rates, and in some cases the equipment as well as the raw material was supplied by the merchant-employer. In such cases the artisans were heavily dependent on the clothier, a dependence that was further increased if they fell into his debt. This "system" certainly operated, broadly speaking, in many towns and villages in 16th century England, but it was very much more varied and complex than this crude outline suggests.

Some clothiers were wealthy men who could deal on level terms with the great London merchants. John Winchcombe and Thomas Dolman could demand of Thomas Gresham large advance payments when they sold him their cloths; lesser men had to content themselves with a down payment in cash with the balance payable in a series of instalments. The widow of Thomas Spring of Lavenham, after paying all her husband's bequests, was still the second wealthiest person in Suffolk in 1523 (after the Duke of Norfolk). But riches on this scale were quite exceptional, and were probably attained by only a handful of individuals. Nor did even the wealthiest of the clothiers find it easy to gain social recognition; in Wiltshire only William Stumpe of Malmesbury was able to win acceptance among the ranks of the country gentry.

It was only these few who could own and run large-scale establishments comparable to the factories of the Industrial Revolution. The doggerel verse of Thomas Deloney has made famous the workshops of John Winchcombe at Newbury:

> Within one room being large and long
> There stood two hundred looms full strong
> Two hundred men the truth is so
> Wrought in these looms all in a row.

Likewise William Stumpe's purchase of Malmesbury Abbey, for conversion into a cloth-factory, has received the greatest possible publicity. But such giant establishments were not the typical units of the Tudor cloth industry, and their contemporary fame is itself indicative of their special status. The industry rested for the most part on the shoulders of humbler men.

Some of these, like John Hedges of Malmesbury or the Langfords of Trowbridge, made quite comfortable fortunes, and they might be accepted among the yeomen of their county, though not among the gentry. They might well own workshops and dyehouses of their own, though not on the grand scale of a Winchcombe or a Stumpe. They might "put out" work to spinners, weavers, fullers and dyers working in their own homes, organising the scattered labour forces of the locality. But even the Hedges and Langfords were pre-eminent in their trade, and from them we move down through a long gradation of lesser men, till we end up with clothiers who were barely distinguishable from the weavers and other craftsmen. At this level a sharp antithesis between clothier and clothworkers is misleading, especially at the beginning of our period. As the number of industrial workers grew, so too did the contrast between employers and employed. But the divisions were often blurred in the 16th century, and a successful weaver might be an employee in relation to a big clothier and at the same time an employer of his fellow-craftsmen. The "domestic system" was capable of infinite variations and combinations.

Not very much is known of the relations between the cloth-producers and the merchants, and the available evidence comes largely from the 1530's and 1540's. This may not be a typical period, since during it the foreign market for cloth was exceptionally good, and the English merchants' eagerness to buy was correspondingly great. And even during this period the account-books of Thomas Kitson and Thomas Gresham show such variety of practice that it is difficult to generalise. The greater clothiers could exact part payment in advance, but not all of them did so. William Stumpe allowed Thomas Gresham to pay £500 in five annual instalments of £100 from 1548-52—a remarkable concession in a time of rapid inflation. Lesser men might normally expect a down-payment of one-half or one-third the purchase price, with the balance paid off in three or six months. It would appear from Gresham's account-book that he paid his debts to the greater clothiers rather more promptly than to the lesser ones; but this may only reflect the fact that the former would have permanent agents in London to collect debts as they fell due, while the latter would have to wait until they next came to London in person. Greater and lesser clothiers alike were willing to accept part payment in goods, and both Kitson and Gresham sometimes settled their accounts partly in cash and partly in woad. But all manner of different arrangements can be found, and the only safe generalisation that can be made is that credit features in nearly all but the very smallest transactions. No interest appears to have been charged—at least overtly—though it is quite possible that the purchase price was raised in proportion to the length of the credit requested. We cannot tell for certain whether this happened, however, or whether varying prices for apparently similar goods were due to pressure of special circumstances or the relative strength of the two parties to the bargain.

In principle all clothiers doing business in London had to sell their wares at Blackwell Hall on certain days of the week. But it is fairly clear that this rule was often evaded, at least in the first part of the century. Kitson regularly made agreements with clothiers to buy all their cloths up to a given date. There is no such clear evidence of pre-contracts by Gresham, but he certainly had regular large-scale dealings with clothiers over long periods, and sometimes paid advances even to small men. In either case it is obvious that bargains were being struck away from Blackwell Hall, and that merchants of the calibre of Kitson and Gresham were not bidding against one another in a public market. They were, on the other hand, eagerly competing for limited supplies before these ever reached London, and their dealings reveal the intensity of demand for cloth in the boom period of the 16th century.

The crisis of 1550–51 hit the clothiers as hard as the merchants, and hit the clothworkers hardest of all. It is unlikely that the crisis was mainly due, as the merchants alleged, to the malpractices of the cloth-producers, though it is possible that hectic efforts to meet an intense demand had led to some shoddy craftsmanship. A lengthy statute of 1552 prescribed in detail for the entire industry, laying down precisely the minimum dimensions and weights of all the commoner types of cloth. This might imply that the government accepted the merchants' case, at least in part. But much more disturbing for the clothiers in the long run was the fact that the boom conditions of the period before 1550 never returned, and that by the end of the century they were facing a rival industry—the New Draperies.

The appearance and growth of these was partly due to the arrival in East Anglia of immigrants from the southern Netherlands, fleeing from Spanish persecution. These Flemish refugees set up the new industry in Norwich and Colchester, just as their compatriots did at Leiden in Holland. At this period improved pasturage in the wool-producing areas of England was producing heavier fleeces with a longer staple; this coarser wool was more suitable for making the light fabrics of the new industry than it was for the traditional broadcloths and kerseys. The change in product was thus partly due to a change in raw material. It was also due in part to the demands of the re-opened English markets in the Mediterranean, and marked a partial change of direction in English trade from northern to southern Europe. The heavy broadcloth had no ready sale in the Mediterranean; the light bays and says sold well. Much the same is true of the Dutch woollen industry, which competed in the Mediterranean with the English manufactures. The two industries had a common origin and a common market.

By the end of the century the new fabrics had conquered East Anglia. Bays and says were being manufactured in Colchester, while Lavenham was making "callimancoes" for export to Russia. They were spreading, too, to the traditional centres of the broadcloth and kersey industry. Bays and serges were appearing in Yorkshire, especially round Halifax. Wiltshire, by the first decade of the 17th century, was turning from its long-established broadcloth manufacture to the making of "Spanish" dyed cloths, and was successful enough to alarm the clothmakers of Holland by this competition. Broadcloths still dominated the English export trade in 1601, when they represented at least three-quarters of its total value. But by 1640 they had lost their ascendancy, and though woollen cloth was still England's only really important export the new stuffs had approached the old in value.

Undoubtedly the coal industry expanded more rapidly than any other during the 16th century. The "vend" from the Newcastle coalfield grew from nearly 33,000 tons in 1564 to nearly 252,000 tons in 1609, while coal imports to London rose from some 24,000 tons in 1586 to 74,000 in 1606. These figures would suggest that the rate or growth was as rapid in the reign of Elizabeth I as during the much more celebrated expansion of the 19th century. Certainly the industry grew faster in England than anywhere else, and it has been estimated that on the eve of the Civil War England produced at least three times as much coal as the whole of Europe. The growth was accompanied by spectacular fortunes for some entrepreneurs, who were able to lease mines from the crown at very modest rents—sometimes a mere thirtieth of their annual value—and by a rapid growth in the East Coast carrying trade. By the end of the century nearly as much shipping was required to bring Newcastle coal to London as was needed for the whole of London's imports from abroad.

Two principal reasons for this great development have been put forward. One was the secularisation of church property, which in the second half of the century made available on favourable terms mining properties that had hitherto not offered an attractive field for investment. In the bishopric of Durham, especially, the crown was willing to permit leases of twenty-one years and longer, where before the bishops had allowed only short-term leases. With the greater security of the longer lease, with the financial inducement of a relatively low rent, and with much reduced interference from the landlord, the entrepreneur was encouraged to put his capital into long-term mining projects that had formerly offered neither safety nor profit. The result was beneficial to the industry, though the financial returns for the crown were inadequate.

The entrepreneurs, however, needed to be assured of a lively demand for their product, not merely a favourable opportunity to produce. This was guaranteed them by an increasingly acute shortage of timber, due both to industrial demand in such industries as iron and shipbuilding and to the growing needs of urban populations, especially London's. In the second half of the century the price of firewood rose much more rapidly than that of most other commodities, and the Londoners were reluctantly overcoming an age-old prejudice against coal as a domestic fuel. Government concern was shown by the crown's attempts to prohibit the taking of timber from the royal forests without special warrant. It is likely that the timber shortage in England came earlier and more acutely than in other European countries, soon to experience the same pressure. For this a rise in population and the demands of other heavy industries seem the most likely explanation. The growth of the coal industry was the effect as well as the cause of parallel growth in other heavy industries.

Among the heaviest consumers of fuel was the iron industry, at this period mainly concentrated in Sussex, Monmouthshire, Glamorganshire and the Forest of Dean. The introduction of the blast-furnace for the production of cast-iron, after about 1540, greatly increased the output of cast-iron—the new furnaces could turn out from 100 to 500 tons a year—but also greatly increased the consumption of timber for charcoal. Coal could not be substituted for charcoal at this stage of the iron industry's development, but the growing timber shortage encouraged such substitution wherever it was technically possible.

Salt-production was one field where this could be done, and the more easily since the cheapest coal was quite adequate for heating pans to evaporate sea-water. At the end of the century this industry became a large-scale enterprise, using great iron pans heated by large furnaces. It was located mainly at the mouth of the Tyne and Wear, where cheap coal was readily accessible. Labour costs were relatively low, but the capital costs quite high. One salt works on the Wear was said in 1589 to have involved an investment of £4000. The use of coal thus concentrated the industry in a particular area, and changed its structure from domestic to capitalistic production. Coal likewise came to be used increasingly in glass-making, in soap-boiling and in brewing, though the rapid and large-scale development of these industries belongs to the early Stuart period, perhaps, rather than the reign of Elizabeth. What all these industries had in common was that their installations demanded a capital outlay well beyond the means of a small craftsman, or even a group of craftsmen. The outlay for one of the new-style blast-furnaces was normally over £1000, the cost of sinking and draining mines for tin and coal might run to much more, once the surface ores had been exhausted. Moreover, since England lacked fast-flowing streams to supply constant and steady water-power, her industries had to employ the more expensive overshot water-wheel to drive the bellows and mills. Hence a need for industrial capital on a scale hitherto unknown, and for the first time rivalling commercial capital in its enterprises.

Most industrial capital came inevitably from the rich merchants of London. It is, however, noteworthy that the Tudor nobility also took a keen interest in business. This went beyond the mere receiving of rents or profits from mines and ironworks on their lands, or fen-drainage on their own estates. It has been estimated that no less than 22 per cent of the Elizabethan aristocratic families owned iron-works, though it must be admitted that many of these preferred to lease their works to a contractor after an initial period of operating the works directly. The nobility showed a willingness to risk their money in coal, iron, lead, alum and glass production that often ran ahead of the more cautious merchants. Even if their total contribution was quantitatively modest, their initiative was important. Their early enterprise in this field, as in that of exploration and colonisation, did something to offset their conspicuous waste of resources in other directions.

All these developments added materially to England's industrial production and established new patterns in its organisation. But their importance must not be exaggerated, and it would be premature to talk of an industrial revolution. The growth of the coal industry in Elizabeth's reign was certainly rapid, but its beginnings were so modest that the percentage increase in the early decades of expansion was bound to be impressive. Mining and metallurgy both made technical advances, but these were often due in the first instance to foreign expertise rather than native inventiveness. English craftsmen showed themselves more apt for mass-production of low-quality wares than for the manufacture of high-grade artistic wares; the glass industry concentrated on windows and bottles of cheap glass, and did not compete with Venetian wares. Some thousands of industrial workers found themselves for the first time concentrated in large-scale enterprises, but these were not yet the norm. No doubt the blast-furnace was more common in the iron industry than was the cloth factory in the textile industry. It was not yet the typical unit of production. Nor had there by 1603 been any substantial shift of population to new areas; the Weald and not the Black Country remained preeminent in iron-production. Nor of course was England remotely an industrial country in depending on industrial exports to pay for imports of food and raw materials. By the end of the 16th century she depended less heavily on German imported metal-ware, and was industrially more self-sufficient. But she was still able, except in the worst harvest years, able to feed herself adequately. It was not yet a case of "export or perish".

Such industrial organisation as existed in 16th century England was supplied by the gilds. These were by no means universal, being confined largely to the towns, and their character and organisation were far from uniform. The century saw some extension of their activities and some moves towards greater uniformity, but even in 1600 it is wrong to imagine that every craft and industry was organised in a gild, or that all gilds adhered to some fixed archetypal pattern. Broad similarities can be discerned and general trends observed, but here again diversity is the order of the day.

By 1485 the craft gilds had evolved a good way since their first establishment. They had never been fully "democratic" in character, nor did they ever resemble at all closely the modern trade union. It is only quite recently that the ordinary industrial labourer has had effective organisations of his own. The employers always tended to dominate the workers; the owners of industrial capital controlled the craftsmen. Within a group of allied trades it was common for one to dominate the others, as was the case with the London Saddlers of the early 14th century, who tried to impose their control over the Painters, Joiners and Lorimers. Characteristically here it was the trading craft dominating the handicrafts. But many of the craft gilds were originally able to treat on a basis of equality, and the dominance of a few of them was not as pronounced as in the Tudor period. Nor had the stratification of individual gilds hardened into a well-defined hierarchy. Their declared aims were the maintenance of respectable standards, achieved mainly through an apprenticeship of varying length; the social welfare of their members, who were helped in time of need by their fellows; in some cases religious duties and functions were added. A less overt aim, though it was probably taken for granted rather than concealed, was to share a limited market equitably among the gild's members. Hence a number of "restrictive practices", which were resented by the few excluded from a trade, but which were not held in general disrepute.

By the 16th century a number of changes had taken place, and these continued through our period. The expansion of both local and foreign markets was dividing the crafts into three distinct groups. The *Discourse of the Common Weal* lists in one group the mercers, grocers, vintners, haberdashers, milliners and "such as do sell wares growing beyond the seas, and do fetch out treasure of the same"; in a second group are placed the craftsmen working for a local town market—the shoemakers, tailors, carpenters, masons, and the members of the victualling trades; into a third group fall the industrial employers—the clothiers, cappers, tanners and worsted makers. The lines of division were not hard and fast, and many successful craftsmen could still engage in trade. But the dominance of the first and third groups was marked, and in London the pre-eminence of the twelve great livery companies reflected the ascendancy of the wealthy wholesalers, many of them active in overseas trade. It was not uncommon for the wealthy member of a lesser London gild to transfer his allegiance to one of the twelve— in spite of the understandable resentment of his spurned fellow-craftsmen. A wide gulf separated the mercer and the shoemaker of Tudor London.

Within many companies the divisions had become much more fixed, and a clearly defined hierarchy had been established. In these only a minority of apprentices ever achieved full membership, the way to the mastership being blocked by exorbitant entrance fees, demands that the candidate pay for a costly and elaborate dinner, or insistence on the production of a "masterpiece" (to show his technical skill) that required months of labour and the use of expensive materials. In face of these restrictions many apprentices became mere journeymen, employees of the wealthier members, eligible only for the Bachelors' organisations which grew up to represent their interests. The son of a wealthy master would normally expect to proceed to the mastership, either directly or after only a brief sojourn in the ranks of the Bachelors. The expectations of the immigrant from the countryside were much less rosy. Unless backed by a substantial patrimony he could not pay the premium demanded for apprenticeship in the greater companies at all; in the lesser companies he was doomed to remain in the middle ranks.

The constitutions of these companies show the formation of inner rings of the wealthiest masters, from whom the Wardens and Courts of Assistants were drawn. These oligarchic bodies devised rules and ordinances for the whole company, though sometimes allowing the Bachelors a restricted right to regulate their own affairs. Not unnaturally

4

they exerted their powers of discipline in a manner conducive to their own interests, and it is difficult not to feel that they often constituted employers' rings, who found in the gild organisation a ready supply of cheap and well-ordered labour for themselves. The seven-year term of apprenticeship, general in London and tending to extend elsewhere, cannot have been necessary for the learning of all crafts. It is only fair to add that the oligarchy was tempered in two ways. Heavy child mortality prevented it from becoming hereditary, and the inner ring constantly changed its composition. In addition a door was left open to the successful craftsman; the London livery companies drew to themselves the more prosperous members of the lesser gilds, while the city ordinances of Norwich compelled any company to admit those who had grown to "abundance of worldly goods and likely to bear worship and estate in the said city". This flexibility both reduced hostility and provided vigorous recruits to the ruling class.

By no means all crafts of the early 16th century showed these tendencies, which appeared most plainly in the wealthier gilds of the larger towns and cities. But such developments were common enough to be typical of the commercial and industrial gilds employing a large labour force, and the hierarchy of apprentice, bachelor and master was familiar. The same three-fold division was to be found in contemporary Paris or Lyon, where the "Compagnon" corresponded to the Bachelor of the English system. In both England and France only the humbler handicrafts retained a relatively democratic structure, and even these were constantly threatened with absorption by aggressive rivals.

The 16th century saw a considerable number of new companies, the majority being created either before about 1520 or after about 1555. Those of the reign of Elizabeth often represent either wholly new industries or industries that had so changed their technical methods as to need new forms of organisation—the Pinners and Stationers of London, for example. London companies often saw a remarkable extension of their area of jurisdiction; the Blacksmiths' charter of 1571 gave them a four-mile circuit in addition to the city and its suburbs. This inevitably accompanied the growth of the capital, itself caused by the overspill of artisans from the city and the immigration of both English craftsmen from the countryside and aliens from further afield. The growing feeling against the last group, for all their great services to English industry, found expression in the anti-alien riots of Evil May Day, 1517.

Antagonism towards foreign workers seems to have diminished after 1517, and was never again so violently expressed. But disputes among and within the gilds remained frequent throughout Elizabeth's reign and continued under the early Stuarts. They arose from the efforts of the town gilds to control workers in suburbs outside the walls, between companies competing in the same market, and between rival classes (usually manufacturers and traders) within the same company. Common to most of them was the problem of lack of direct contact between maker and consumer, and the former's dependence on a middleman to sell his wares. The frequent legislation for the leather industry, especially in the years 1548–55, arose largely from the rivalry of the London Cordwainers and Curriers with one another, and also the desire of the wealthy traders in both companies to control the native and alien craftsmen of the suburbs. What appears to be a series of unsteady experiments by a faltering government was in fact a wavering struggle between two powerful pressure groups. The craftsmen's resentment of control by the wealthy traders was sometimes satisfied by their gaining independence; the Feltmakers escaped the tutelage of the Haberdashers and the Glovers that of the Leathersellers, for example. But others, such as the Artisan Clothworkers, failed to win their freedom, and in general the custom of London was unfavourable to the movement. That custom upheld the right of any freeman in any company to practise the trade of any other. This benefited the wealthy trader, who could deploy his wealth where he wished—at the cost of less strict discipline in his own company. It was disadvantageous to the small craftsman, who could not form an effective monopoly in his own field. And while some vigorous crafts gained independence, others became amalgamated with one another. One such process of amalgamation was completed at Gloucester in 1607, when the goldsmiths, pewterers, brasiers, coppersmiths, wiredrawers, cardmakers, pinmakers and plumbers formed a Company of Metalworkers. This in part represented the obliteration of decaying industries, though the pin-makers did not fall into that category and soon made the city a centre of pin manufacture.

There is also evidence of sharp conflicts inside the companies, and of keen resentment against the ruling oligarchs. In 1540 a London Clothworker complained that members of the Court of Assistants regularly evaded the laws against exporting unfinished cloth, adding darkly that there were already many heads set on London Bridge, and if there were three or four more it would make no matter. Some twenty years later a Pewterer told his governing body, "You have ruled a good while. I pray God that you have not ruled too long, and that the company have not occasion to curse you for your government." And in 1601 another embittered Clothworker was removed from the Livery for declaring that the Assistants "were Pelicans, and did suck out the blood of their dam and weed out the profit of the Company's lands, which of right belonged and was given to them of the handitrade of the company." But such emotional utterances probably did little to disturb the serenity of the ruling groups. Secure in the support of the City authorities—who found them a convenient instrument for keeping public order—they were unshaken by any serious revolution. In most of the greater companies their wealth and authority advanced hand in hand.

The London Livery Companies are the best-documented gilds of the 16th century, as well as its wealthiest and most powerful. They had their counterparts in the larger towns where similar conflicts arose. Yet there still survived at the end of the century companies that preserved some measure of egalitarianism and resisted the dominance of the large-scale enterprise. The Shoemakers of Chester were shop-keepers and therefore men of some substance; but they for-bade their members in 1609 to have goods made in the country or to open more than one shop. They were thus still resisting both the encroachments of the domestic system and the rise of the over-mighty member.

The domestic system of industry, most prominent in the cloth trade, was in the long run the most serious enemy of all the gilds. The very success of the gilds in imposing mono-polies in the towns encouraged those who set up new indus-tries to do so in the countryside, where gild restrictions could be evaded. A number of new industries in the period—iron-manufacture, coal-mining, large-scale salt-panning—either could not be located inside the towns or were not adaptable to the gild structure. The Apprentices' Act of 1563, which attempted to generalise that structure for Eng-lish industry, came too late to arrest this process, and may even have accelerated it. The new industries grew up either in the country or in towns where gilds were not too powerful, and the future lay with the capitalist entrepreneur operating in a relatively free labour market. There were no gilds in Birmingham or Wolverhampton, and the apprenticeship clauses of the 1563 Act were not enforced in Warwickshire or Worcestershire. By 1603 even the London Livery Com-panies were past their peak, and never again enjoyed the ascendancy they had held in the early years of the century. Though still powerful, they already had a slightly archaic air. A century later they had served their turn. Their passing was not an unmixed blessing, even for the humbler artisans who had felt their discipline most acutely. At their most oli-garchic and tyrannical they had still afforded some protec-tion and corporate fellowship. Deprived of these safeguards the industrial worker had to await the coming of the 19th century trade union to enjoy a comparable security.

The towns in which the gilds had their being underwent varying fortunes. A number were decayed at the beginning of the century, and were in serious economic and financial difficulties. In Lincoln houses were falling empty, and disused churches were being pulled down on the orders of the city council, the fabric being appropriated to the city's use. A similar destruction of churches took place in York, while Norwich was very slow to repair the damage caused by a great fire in the 1530's. Bristol and Coventry are reported to be economically stagnant in the middle years of the century. Not all contemporary lamentations can be taken at their face value, since the plea of poverty was often used to support a request for a reduction in tax or rent. But the government was concerned enough to pass a series of statutes in 1536–42 to enjoin the rebuilding of decayed parishes, and the testimony of travellers like Leland is emphatic. Some of these towns were suffering from a decline in the trades that had brought them prosperity in earlier times. Lincoln had lost its great trade in wool, and had become a city of lesser tradesmen. Coventry, said the author of the *Discourse of the Common Weal*, was failing to compete with its foreign rivals in the production of thread. Nearly all the ports of the realm were losing trade to London, and from 1500 their foreign trade actually declined while the total rose. And they were losing not only trade but also men; more and more the enterprising young man sought his fortune in London rather than a provincial town or city. The capital, and contemporaries were quick to note and resent it, grew in wealth and population at the expense of the others. It was a poor consolation that to the subsidy of 1534–35 London contributed as much as all the other towns of England put together.

In some cases the decay was arrested by the development of a new trade or industry in place of the old. The "New Draperies" at Norwich were a more than adequate substitute for the fallen worsted industry. Coventry turned to the manufacture of pins. The East Anglian ports found new wealth in the coastal trade and in the shipping industry. Exeter thrived on the French trade, and could thus afford to leave the Netherlands and German markets to the Merchant Adventurers of London. Newcastle's booming coal industry likewise compensated its merchants for their exclusion from the Adventurers' monopoly.

The sixteenth century also saw the emergency of some new towns with a spectacular future before them. By 1600 Manchester was said to be the most populous town in Lancashire, though that was no great achievement in such a thinly populated country. Birmingham, as yet only 2000 strong, and whose wealthiest men were tanners, not ironmongers, was just beginning its climb to greatness. The rise of Plymouth balanced the decline of Southampton. A number of market towns—Torrington, Honiton and Tavistock in Devon, Melton Mowbray and Loughborough in Leicestershire, to name only a few—were flourishing centres of local trade. By the end of Elizabeth's reign town life was more flourishing than it had been a hundred years before. Not all the old centres had recovered the ground lost, and the dominance of London was even more pronounced in 1603 than in 1485. But the clear evidence of townsmen's wills and inventories, and of the surviving buildings, as well as the powerful inference of rising urban populations, all indicate a revival of prosperity and of the attractive powers of the Tudor towns and cities.

The century saw numerous charters of incorporation granted or regranted. These were a symbol and guarantee of the town's status and independence, and a useful weapon in the unending disputes between towns and local landed magnates or officials. From the government's point of view they were a pledge of good behaviour, since what had been granted could as easily be withdrawn. The balance of gain was probably on the side of the town, since independence was fiercely cherished both for practical reasons and more intangible ones of esteem. Since even the wealthiest provincial burgher never had the same political influence or social standing as a landed gentleman, he was all the more anxious to assert his authority and dignity in his own sphere. Certainly Tudor aldermen were as touchy and sensitive about their position as any knight or esquire.

The government of most towns and cities was intensely oligarchic, and was almost invariably concentrated in the hands of a very few leading merchants. A typical case is that of Exeter, where from 1500 the council of twenty-four ceased to be elected annually and became a self-co-opting body. The Freemen of the city had a choice in the appointment of the Mayor—but only between two candidates nominated by the council. Since the mayor was invariably one of the twenty-four, each of whom had therefore some prospects of nomination in his turn, democracy and tyranny were alike excluded. It was typical also that the constitution of 1500 was officially confirmed in 1509 by a privy seal writ of Henry VIII; the crown showed itself consistently favourable to restricted franchises, and though its interventions in civic affairs were not invariably on the side of a particular ruling group, the general trend was towards co-option rather than free elections. Norwich, with its Common Council of sixty members, was exceptionally democratic by 16th century standards.

Most towns were in some financial difficulties during this period. In some cases this was due to falling population and economic decline. More often it was caused by the assumption of wider social responsibilities, while all municipalities were caught in the cleft stick of fixed incomes from rents and rising prices. Lincoln found it hard to pay the fee-farm of £180 to the crown, especially since £100 of it had been alienated to the Roos family, and only after long controversy was this liability redeemed from the third earl of Rutland for £300 in 1574. The total receipts of Leicester in 1558–59 were just under £58. Exeter's budget showed a deficit in most years during Elizabeth's reign, and its income only twice exceeded £1000. The cost of salaries and perquisites had risen from £90 in 1549–50 to £274 in 1602–03. Some of this may have been due to the spirit of extravagance that rebuilt the Guildhall at a cost of £789 in 1593–96, but most was due to increasing professionalisation in town administration at a time of rising costs and wages. In towns like these there was little or no margin to meet unforeseen expenditure, and special levies or loans had to be raised to meet unexpected bills. In Exeter a liability of high office was to become perforce a creditor of the city; John Periam was owed £317 at the end of his receivership in 1582, and it was four years before he was paid off. Everywhere civic office meant financial loss for the holder in the short run, though there were indirect gains to be made from controlling a town's economic life.

The first responsibility of town governments was to keep order, with special vigilance shown towards alien immigrants and sturdy vagabonds. Most of them showed a strong concern for public morality, sins (such as fornication) being punished as crimes. A Puritan disapproval of the most robust popular amusements is creeping in at the end of the century, compensated a little by increased aldermanic pomp and pageantry. In a hierarchically ordered male society it is not surprising to find that punishments fell exclusively on the lower orders, and more heavily on the woman than on the man.

Most muncipalities were much preoccupied with the regulation of food prices, a problem not unconnected with that of public order. This was the more necessary when prices fluctuated violently over short periods; wheat stood at 12s. 6d. the quarter at Lincoln in June, 1520, and was reported at 24s. in the following February. In time of dearth a common device was to raise a loan or levy to buy grain in bulk and sell it to the poor at cost price. In 1555 Exeter raised £500 to purchase rye for its citizens. It was characteristic, too, that Lincoln paid special attention to the victualling gilds in the extensive revision of gild charters that took place in the 1550's and 1560's; detailed regulations were laid down for prices, measures and the conditions of apprenticeship. Other common articles of consumption that were controlled in

4*

price included candles, fuel and building materials. The poorer citizens were thus at least partly cushioned against sharp and sudden increases.

Regular provision for the poor—beyond the removal of rogues and "foreigners"—was another charge on the towns. Private charity often ran ahead of civic care in providing both almshouses and casual doles for the poor, and both anticipated the efforts of the national government. Norwich had a comprehensive scheme in operation by the 1570's. In 1551 four aldermen of Lincoln took the initiative in trying to provide work for the poor of that city. Land and premises were made available cheaply, and a number of promoters were to set idle young people to work at weaving cloth. But seven years later it was found that few if any broadcloths had been produced by this scheme, which had clearly failed of its purpose. Exeter parishes were poorly endowed for charitable purposes, though an indirect way of relieving poverty was practised in the form of the revolving loan fund —money lent to artificers or young merchants for a limited period of years to enable them to set up in business. One such fund, established in 1568, provided £300 to be lent out in sums of £5 to £20. But Exeter was one city where government action was probably necessary to effect more regular provision. By 1563 this was being made, and expenditure on poor relief had reached £119. Following the Act of 1576 the city eventually set up a bridewell (or workhouse) in 1579, a permanent governor being appointed in 1593. It is not clear how effective the relief proved to be, but Exeter and other cities were doing something to ease the distress of those who could not themselves save against sickness, trade depression and unemployment.

The cost of bearing the dignity of office and liability to compulsory loans without interest were two of the drawbacks of membership of the urban ruling class. Dignity and prestige no doubt compensated in part, but there could be more material advantages as well. The 1560 charter of the **Exeter Merchant Adventurers** gave members of the new company a monopoly in the wholesale trade in overseas commodities. It was not so restrictive a charter as the one sought by the city authorities in 1559, since it left open the retail trade and made it possible for any artisan to join the company within the next three years if he gave up his craft. But clearly it represented a victory for the greater merchants of the city, and it had been strenuously opposed by the artisans, led by the tailors. It was a trifle disingenuous of Hooker, the city's persuasive spokesman to the central government, to make out the new company was comparable to the traditional craft gild. In effect the council had used its power and influence to obtain a vital monopoly for its own members and their kin.

Not all councils had the same opportunities for self-enrichment, but it is true that the inequalities of wealth were most pronounced in the more thriving towns and cities. At Exeter only just over six per cent of those contributing to the subsidy of 1523–24 were assessed at £40 or more in goods, and only twenty per cent in all were assessed at £10 or more. The wealthier citizens no doubt escaped relatively lightly in the assessment, but making all possible allowances for this fact it is still clear that only a small minority of the citizens were even moderately well-to-do. The Leicester subsidy of 1544 also shows just under twenty per cent assessed at £10 or over. (A significant feature of the Leicester figures is that five persons were assessed at exactly £40 but no-one above that sum.) In both cities those assessed at less than £2 in goods or wages amounted to sixty per cent of the contributors. In both cities it is further safe to assume that one-third of those assessed were found to own or earn less than the £1 minimum, and therefore were not taxed at all. The Exeter figures suggest that the city's rich men made a greater contribution to the subsidy than those of Leicester. (At Norwich and Bristol their share was even higher.) But they could well afford it: a mere three per cent of the contributors owned half the assessed property, and this is probably an understatement. In extreme contrast to these wealthy few, at least half the population lived in grinding poverty, at or below the level of subsistence. From these taxation records alone it is easy to see that strict discipline and the relief of famine were necessary, and went hand in hand with each other.

Other sources show the same extremes. Exeter merchants did not rival those of London in wealth, and only about one-third of surviving inventories for the period 1540–1640 show estates of more than £2000. But prosperous traders could probably expect an annual income of over £100 at a time when the lesser Devonshire gentry drew only between £50 and £100 from their lands. Their three-story houses, with comfortably furnished hall, parlour, four or five sleeping chambers and domestic offices, contrasted with the single-room hovels of the poorer artisans. The better houses in Leicester were usually of only two stories, and less luxuriously appointed. But there is still a wide gulf between the house of the wealthy butcher Philip Freake (whose inventory totalled £625), with its hall, parlour, kitchen, buttery, nether parlour, six chambers, and ample shop accommodation—and the modest dwelling of the shoemaker John Darker (inventory £7) with only hall, parlour, kitchen and shop. It is indicative of living standards in Leicester that in 1559 a labourer's cottage could be built for just under £5. A single room with the sparsest possible furnishing was all that the Tudor poor could expect.

Only the more solid and impressive of Tudor houses have survived to our own day, and it is their owners who have left the most abundant written record of their way of life. It would be dangerous to conclude from such evidence that all was well with the townships of England in 1600, even in those which had recovered from the depression of the earlier years of the century. A thriving trade brought wealth and comfort to only a tiny minority. These were the favoured few who ruled over their own communities, intermarried within their own circle, and transmitted their wealth and power to their children. The oligarchies were not completely closed, and indeed they had to refresh their blood with new members all through the century. But by its end more sons were succeeding their fathers in business, and leading families were surviving longer in civic life. The oligarchies were not only small but were increasingly hereditary. At the opposite end of the social scale lay more than half the other townsfolk. Their lot had always been a hard one, and by the end of the Tudor period it was actually becoming harder. Rapidly soaring food prices rose far more than the wages of the town artisan who lived on his wages, and there is little doubt that his standard of living deteriorated sharply if not catastrophically. Further removed from the soil, the urban labourer was worse off than his agrarian counterpart in time of harvest failure and acute dearth. It was on this submerged class that the first and harshest impact of the famines of the 1590's fell, and even the better-organised urban charities of Elizabeth's reign can have softened the blow but little. The fine houses and civic pageantry of Norwich and Exeter represent only the tip of the ice-berg. There was a darker and grimmer underside to their prosperity.

London cannot be considered along with the other towns; it stood quite alone. It completely dwarfed them in size of population, in economic and political power. A conservative estimate of its population in 1600 puts it at 150,000, and other estimates range as high as 300,000. It was probably more than ten times the size of Norwich, the second-largest city of England, and perhaps twenty times the size of any other city. In contrast to its older rivals it had grown, and was still growing, at a prodigious rate. On any estimate of its population, numbers tripled in the course of the 16th century. Its preponderant share in the country's overseas trade was no doubt a major factor in this growth. Practically speaking, trade in the most lucrative markets—first at Antwerp and later in the monopoly areas of the new trading companies—was confined to Londonders, to the sons and apprentices of freemen of the livery companies. It was in London that the great mercantile fortunes of the age were made, the wealth of its leading citizens exceeding that of the Bristol or Hull merchants by as much as their wealth outstripped that of the traders of a small market town. It is true that the fortunes of even a Richard Gresham or Thomas Sutton did not compare with those of a great landed aristocrat—no more did the wealth of the Exeter merchants measure up to that of the greater Devonshire landowners. But the opportunities offered to the ambitious young provincial were immensely greater than those of the outports or county towns. It was to be expected that London would attract not only the trade of the country but also its up-and-coming traders.

Overcrowding and insanitary conditions, with consequent severe epidemics, meant that London could not even maintain its population without considerable immigration. That it was able to increase three-fold in a hundred years argues a truly massive influx of new recruits. This can be clearly demonstrated from the evidence of London wills in the period. In the years 1480–1660 only fourteen out of 172 mayors were London born, while of 403 wealthy testators classified by W. K. Jordan as "great merchants" less than ten per cent are known to have been born in the city. Of 813 liveried merchants only 75 (nine per cent) were natives of London, and of 389 shopkeepers and retailers less than four per cent. The upper ranks of the merchant class seem to have been recruited from three main areas—from the western counties (especially Shropshire and Staffordshire); from four east-coast counties stretching southwards from Yorkshire; and from the Home Counties. The shopkeepers came more predominantly from the last area only. It can be suggested that about one-third to one-half of the immigrants had some family connection with trade or industry. The son of a wealthy provincial merchant or prosperous artisan would struggle to raise the £10 premium demanded of a great company like the Goldsmiths, or at least the £1 or £2 required by the lesser gilds. Along with them came an even larger number of young men whose previous connections had been with the land. Perhaps about half of these were drawn from the yeomen, and the rest in equal proportions from the gentry and husbandmen, but these terms are so elastic that we cannot be precise about social origins.

Not all London immigrants aimed to make a fortune in trade, though we must add to the incoming apprentices a substantial number of alien settlers. In the upper social brackets were also those who came to make their career in the law, or to try their luck at Court; here again the opportunies were concentrated in the capital, and increasingly so. Among the humbler arrivals were numbers of domestic servants, casual labourers and discharged soldiers, whose unstable economic position presented a growing problem to the authorities. To some extent all Tudor towns tended to draw on the surrounding countryside, since urban mortality was normally higher than that in country districts. But the demands of London were much more voracious than those of any other towns, and its economic attractions much more insistent. Well might the Bristol merchants complain to James I that it was "as if God had no sons to whom He gave the benefit of the earth but in London."

The problems of London were no different in kind from those of other cities, but immensely greater in scope. It was fortunate in possessing a governing body with real authority behind it—the mayor and aldermen enjoyed the support of both the Privy Council above and the wardens of the companies below—and a merchant class with a powerfully developed sense of social responsibility. They did not, it is true, plan the development of the city in a systematic way; but it would be anachronistic to expect that of any 16th century city government. The dissolution of the monasteries helped to ease the pressure on space and accommodation, but it was wealthy private speculators like Sir Robert Rich, the grantee of the priory of St. Bartholomew's, Smithfield, who took the initiative in filling the blank spaces with tenements and made their own fortunes in the process. The city was perpetually spilling out at the edges, Southwark being absorbed in the reign of Edward VI, and Kent being encroached upon by the end of the century. Proclamations and

statutes in the 1590's failed to prevent indiscriminate building within a three-mile radius of the city boundaries, and the
great sprawl continued.

But civic and private enterprise did combine to alleviate,
if not solve, the social problems of poverty, unemployment
and sickness. The city shamed Henry VIII and Edward VI
into founding the five royal hospitals—St. Bartholomew's,
St. Thomas's, Christ's Hospital, Bridewell and Bedlam. Its
richest merchants endowed well-organised charities on an
unprecedented scale, and their carefully regulated almshouses provided a pattern for the rest of the country. The
Londoners moreover made a direct contribution of impressive size to other parts of the realm. Nearly one-third of
London's charitable donations went to counties other than
Middlesex. Both inside and outside London the favoured
charities were markedly secular in character. While merchant wealth went to support almshouses, schools and the
two universities, the spire of St. Paul's, destroyed by fire in
1561, was never rebuilt. John Stow, the devoted chronicler
and topographer of his native city, laments again and again
the destruction of churches and religious monuments. But
his great *Survey of London* (1598) is as much a eulogy of secular
achievement as a lament for vanished splendours. And certainly the material needs of London's citizens were extremely
pressing. If we may assume a distribution of wealth and
poverty such as we have met in Exeter and Leicester, then
we must suppose that by 1600 at least 100,000 Londoners
were at best scraping a bare subsistence and at worst suffering
actual starvation. A survey of the 1590's suggests that only
some 4000 required poor relief, but any official estimate
would tend to minimise the problem, and it is unlikely that
even in prosperous London the destitute amounted to only
two per cent of the population. If we accept such an optimistic calculation, it remains true that there were large
numbers on the very edge of disaster, while the extremes of
wealth and poverty were more glaringly apparent than in
any provincial city. An enormous gulf divided the rich

merchant of Milk Street from the slum-dweller of South-wark. It is some measure of the authority and charity of London's rulers that these contrasts did not express themselves in overt class-warfare, and that after 1517 there were no major social riots inspired by economic discontent or oppression.

At the death of Elizabeth I England's industry was more diverse than it had been when her dynasty took the throne. Coal and iron had assumed a new importance, and large capital installations were more common. But woollen cloth was still the country's major export, and the new developments had brought deforestation but not depopulation to the traditional industrial areas. In the towns the framework of gild organisation remained strong, but outside their walls both the older textile manufacture and the newer heavy industries were escaping its control. There had been a recovery from the urban depression of Henry VIII's reign, but its fruits went mainly to a small circle of merchants that dominated the life of every town. For the humbler towns-folk the 1590's had been years of real hardship, and their standard of living was lower than it had been a century before. London had increased its ascendancy, and complaints of its monstrous growth were loud and widespread. But the pattern of town life had not changed so very much during a century of Tudor rule. The challenge of the new industrial cities still lay a long away ahead.

IV

PRICES AND SOCIAL CHANGE

A POTENT CAUSE of urban and other changes was the major rise in prices that occurred during the 16th and early 17th centuries. Some historians have been so impressed by it as to write of a "price revolution". But the extent of it is a matter of debate, so hard is it to construct a reliable index for even one commodity—let alone several—and the causes and results of it are even more controversial. Since its importance cannot be denied, the difficulties must be faced. Only rather tentative answers can be offered, but we can at least try to define the limits and nature of the movement, and trace the more important economic and social consequences.

Our knowledge of 16th century prices is inadequate in many ways. The evidence is meagre, and what we have is scattered and hard to interpret. For some common commodities—butter and cheese, for example—there is very little evidence indeed. For others, such as woollen cloth and other textiles, there is a fair amount of evidence, but this is not detailed enough to help us. Sizes and qualities varied very greatly, and they are not specified often enough for us to compare the prices of comparable goods. Cereals, for which the evidence is more abundant than most commodities, varied in price from year to year with the harvests, and even from district to district in the same year. Almost the only commodity for which we have copious price-material is wheat, and this was not the staple food of the bulk of the population. Too much concentration on wheat-prices may give a misleading impression of Tudor standards of living. When the price of wheat doubled in a bad harvest-year the poorer classes did not automatically starve—they ate a higher proportion of the cheaper cereals instead. Since the price of these would almost certainly rise at the same time as that of wheat, they were undoubtedly worse off and their food fell off in both quality and quantity; but not necessarily to the catastrophic extent suggested by the wheat figures.

Further difficulties arise when we try to assess changes in the standard of living of the Tudor population. This can only be done by imagining a standard Tudor family, estimating its regular consumption of basic foods and other consumer goods, and measuring this against changes in price of the main articles. We know so little about the size and distribution of the Tudor population that the hypothesis of a standard family is very arbitrary. The selection of its regular articles of consumption is even more arbitrary. It is often imposed upon us quite simply by the information available on prices. We can take little account of changing tastes, and in the main we have to assume that the family of 1485 ate and dressed much the same as the family of 1603. This assumption may not be too wide of the mark for the mass of the population, who lived near the level of subsistence and therefore had little choice. It is less valid for the wealthier classes, who clearly (from the evidence of their wills and inventories) raised their standards as time went on. To make too much of all these difficulties, however, would simply be to admit defeat, and we must make what we can of our evidence in spite of the obstacles. At the same time an emphatic warning must be given that no 16th century composite price-index has the accuracy and reliability of the 20th century cost of living index, and our conclusions must be cautious. The most we can hope for is a general impression of the way of life of a humble family that barely makes both ends meet.

The most satisfactory price-index so far produced is that compiled in 1956 by E. H. Phelps Brown and Sheila V. Hopkins, which covers the whole period 1264–1954. It is not a comprehensive cost-of-living index of the modern type, but the next best thing in the circumstances. It is based on articles normally consumed by a family living in Southern England, mainly foodstuffs but including also some manufactured goods such as textiles. The make-up of the "family shopping basket" is adjusted from time to time in the light of known habits of consumption—potatoes take the place of peas in the 19th century, for example. The index thus deals only with the basic necessities of life, and is no guide to the cost of living of the rich merchant or landlord. But it does give a rough clue to the rising expenses of the majority of the population, who could make few purchases not comprised in the basic list.

The base period for the index is 1451–75—the end of a long period of relatively stable prices. The index figure 100 therefore represents the average price of the "basket" during those years. The index continues to hover about the 100 level until the year 1510, when the great Tudor inflation may be said to begin. There is first a sharp rise up to 1521, when the index figure briefly reaches 167, followed by a more stable period up to the early 1540's, when the figures fluctuate about the 150 mark. Then comes a very rapid rise to over 200 in the later 1540's, to 270 in 1555, 370 in 1556 and 409 in 1557. After this phenomenal peak there is a marked drop to only 230 in 1558, but thereafter a steadier rise resumes. By 1570 the 300 mark had again been reached, and in the 1580's the level varies about 340. A really violent rise came in the 1590's, the figures for the last few years of the century reading:

1594	..	381
1595	..	515
1596	..	505
1597	..	685
1598	..	579
1599	..	474
1600	..	459

A series of exceptionally bad harvests was largely responsible for this new peak. But the level never drops below 400 again, and is normally over 500 in the years 1610–30. It seems fair to suggest, therefore, that the prices of basic consumables had at least tripled by 1580 and quadrupled by 1600. How had this come about?

The most popular and widespread explanation of the price-rise, found in innumerable text-books, attributes it in the main to European imports of American silver. This is an extension to English history of the theories of Earl J. Hamilton, who found an apparently close correlation between rising prices in Spain and imports of American silver at Seville. The argument that the rise was *due* to the silver imports is in fact only partly valid even for Spain. It is a very dangerous and misleading argument when applied to 16th century England. In the first place silver imports to Spain reach a significant volume only after 1545, the year of the discovery of the fabulous mine at Potosi in Peru. They cannot therefore help us to explain why prices in England had already doubled by the mid-century. In the second half of the century, it is true, silver came into Spain in ever-growing quantities, reaching a peak in the 1590's. This no doubt had a considerable impact on prices in Spain, but before we can use it to explain the price-rise in England we have to explain how Spanish silver got to England, or how rising prices abroad forced up those at home. English privateers did make some lucky hauls, but hardly so many as to distort the whole economy, and there seems to be no evidence of continuous large-scale bullion imports. A favourable trade-balance might have produced this, but it is unlikely that the trade-balance in the 16th century was ever so favourable as to produce a significant inflow of specie. If such an inflow had taken place the price of silver at the Mint would have fallen, and no such fall in fact occurred. Since, too, the import trade dealt largely in luxuries or near-luxuries, it seems unlikely that rising prices across the Channel could of themselves have produced a five-fold increase in grain prices in England. Indeed the fact that grain prices rose faster than either industrial prices or wages tells strongly against the whole theory. Some part of the English "price revolution" may fairly be attributed to monetary inflation radiating from Seville, but this cannot be made the mainspring.

Probably a more important long-term factor was growth of population with consequent pressure on limited resources that failed to grow as quickly. The difficulty here is that we have no accurate statistics of the Tudor population, and for the moment this explanation can be no more than a likely hypothesis. Historians are, however, agreed that some increase did occur, and that this was most marked in the towns. The population of London in particular may have risen from 50,000 to 200,000 during the 16th century, though these figures are of necessity very tentative. Certainly London was making very great demands on the food-supplies of its hinterland, and similar pressure was exerted by other cities such as Bristol or Norwich. Increased urban populations would explain why food prices fluctuated more and more violently with good or bad harvests in the later years of the century, and why wages failed to keep pace with prices.

The great debasement of the 1540's was undoubtedly another important factor. Between 1543 and 1551 the silver content of the coinage was reduced by more than two-thirds. The mid-century uprush of prices was clearly in part due to this. The deflationary efforts of the government in 1551 (calling down the currency to half its face value) had only a temporary effect on the movement, which did not reach a new stability till the 1560's. Though debasement was not the only inflationary factor of these middle years, Henry VIII, Somerset and Northumberland clearly have much to answer for.

Heavy government expenditure might also tend to push up prices. The cost of government, in England as elsewhere, rose progressively as administration became more elaborate. As, however, many administrative posts, especially local ones, were unpaid, or were paid indirectly in the form of fees and perquisites, this factor alone would not have been serious. It was war that drastically increased the expense of government, and compelled heavy borrowing as well, and such expenditure had the further disadvantage of being economically unproductive for the most part. Government spending was no doubt slight by modern standards, and its inflationary effect only marginal. But it is at least interesting that the Tudor inflation first began when the peace policy of Henry VII gave place to the war policy of his son, that the inflationary 1540's were also war years, and that the even more hectic 1590's were the years of the Spanish war and the Irish rebellion.

Easier credit and more rapid circulation of currency and

credit instruments would also be inflationary. It is unfortunately quite impossible to show the extent of such a development. The heavy sales of monastic lands in the 1540's activated the land-market and speeded circulation. Bills of exchange, both for normal trading and for speculation became more widely used, and borrowing on the security of land more common. The great financier-speculator, a Thomas Gresham or a Horatio Pallavicino, is an Elizabethan rather than a Henrician phenomenon. But it may be that we simply have more evidence for the later period, and it would certainly be a mistake to imagine that the early Tudor merchants lacked adequate credit facilities or lived in a state of financial innocence. Once more we can offer only a tentative suggestion.

It has sometimes been alleged that those who bought up monastic lands proved themselves harsh landlords and rack-rented their tenants. It would be difficult to show that this took place on a large scale, or that in general lay landlords were worse than ecclesiastical ones. It is true that widespread rack-renting would have the effect of raising the price of agricultural produce, since tenants would be forced to try to sell as dearly as they could. There is evidence that some landlords pushed up rents more than was warranted by rising prices, but we cannot say how general this was. In many counties fixed rents and numerous freeholds restricted such activities. It is in any case doubtful whether rack-rented tenants could significantly force up prices, or were more prone to ignore the "just" price than others; the law of supply and demand was more potent, and harvests did more than landlords to determine prices.

There is, in short, no fully convincing explanation of the great Tudor price-rise in the present state of our knowledge. Of the various hypotheses offered, a rise in population is perhaps the most likely and important. But without census figures this cannot be demonstrated; nor can the possible impact of government spending, currency debasement, easier credit or harsh landlordism be accurately assessed.

Their very existence is open to question. The inflation thus remains a largely unexplained phenomenon. Our meagre evidence of prices and the plaintive cries of contemporaries leave us in no doubt that it did take place.

Can the price-rise fairly be called a "revolution"? To those who have lived through the much more rapid inflation of the 20th century a four-fold increase in prices spread over ninety years will not appear sensational. The Brown-Hopkins index shows for our own time a nearly four-fold rise in forty years. But the 16th century inflation was more drastic than any before the most modern period, and came after a century of comparative stability. In our age, too, society is more adaptable than in the Tudor era, and past experience as well as a more developed system of government control work to mitigate its effects. In a more rigid economy, where both custom and law hindered change and adjustment, the impact of rapid inflation was more violent and less easily mitigated. All those who lived on fixed incomes, whether from rents or their own toil, suffered acutely. Those whose position and talents allowed them to take advantage of changing conditions were able to weather the storm. The favoured and the victims were to be found in all classes, though the range of opportunity varied.

At the top of the social hierarchy stood the peerage, generally alluded to as "nobility" by contemporaries. Their titles and social pre-eminence derived from aristocratic descent or present wealth and services. Though some were immensely wealthy, and though newly created peers were sometimes granted lands to enable them to maintain the dignity of their titles, they were not an economically distinct class; a peerage did not necessarily imply vast riches. They were those whom the kings had chosen to honour. Under Henry VII and Henry VIII they were often chosen for political and administrative services to the crown; this is true of 25 out of 39 families raised to the peerage in the years 1485–1547. Elizabeth I was more reluctant to reward such services in this way, and William Cecil was the only peer created for his services; Walsingham, Knollys and Hatton had to be content with knighthoods. Her new peers acquired nobility rather in virtue of their local standing in the counties, where the wealth acquired in trade, the law and (more rarely) farming gave them an influence that could be useful to the crown. Services were certainly expected of them, but the titles were granted with an eye to future utility rather than past good work. Though they were no longer all the counsellors of the crown—in particular they did not have automatic access to the Privy Council—they could still be useful as military commanders, as political props to the monarch in and out of parliament, and as ornaments of a brilliant court.

Their numbers remained remarkably constant during the 16th century. There were 55 peers in 1485 and the same number in 1597, with only slight variations in between. But the turn-over was rapid, and constant replacements were necessary. In the period 1485–1547 thirty noble families passed out of the peerage through natural causes in addition to thirteen removed (at least temporarily) by attainder. The mortality of the peerage under the earlier Tudors was quite as rapid as that during the Wars of the Roses. It slowed down under Elizabeth, but throughout the 16th century we are dealing with a class that changed its composition at a great rate.

It is undoubtedly true that the peerage, as a group, lost power and influence in the Tudor period, though the loss was relative rather than absolute. They did not dominate the central government, and had access to it only when the crown chose to call for their assistance. Their military importance also declined. Though high commands in time of war regularly went to great lords—Leicester in the Netherlands or Essex in Ireland—and though in the first half of the century the retinues of the peers and other landed magnates were still of some importance, by the reign of Elizabeth the peers had ceased to supply a significant element to the Tudor army or to represent a serious risk to the crown. They could not command private armies of their tenants and retainers, and depended for their prestige on the clienteles that they advanced or protected by their local or court influence. It is perhaps for this reason that the term "baron", with its connotations of turbulence and military violence, passes out of use in the 16th century; both contemporaries and later historians talk instead of the "nobles", though there is no warrant for an abrupt change of terminology at the year 1485. Above all, the peers had lost ground to the substantial gentry and lay officers. Was this the reflection or result of a weakened economic position?

In recent years there has been a lively controversy on this last point. The argument put forward first by Professor R. H. Tawney and later supported by Mr. Lawrence Stone is that between 1540 and 1640 the aristocracy lost ground in face of rising prices and failed to adjust to the needs of the time. As a class they were too old-fashioned to improve their estates so as to obtain the greatest possible income from them, and at the same time unwilling to cut their expenses to fit their reduced incomes. Faced with mounting deficits and debts they were forced to sell part of their estates, and the beneficiaries of this process were the more go-ahead owners of medium-sized estates, who applied to land the business-like procedures they had learned in trade or the law. The result was a substantial net swing, both of capital and income, from the aristocracy to the gentry. Thence, it is argued, followed a change in the balance of political power. The outcome of the civil war merely set the seal on a change that had already taken place.

It is not difficult, of course, to produce evidence of conspicuous extravagance among the peers. They spent vast sums on building their great houses, and the style of these became more extravagant in the course of the century. There is Burghley, with his houses at Burghley, Theobalds and Waltham; Suffolk builds Audley End and the Countess of Shrewsbury builds Hardwick Hall. The ninth Earl of Northumberland spends over £5000 on Syon. Extravagant households also took their toll. The Derby household expenses ran to nearly £3000 in 1561, and the estate servants number 140 in 1590—to support a family of five. Equally populous was the Berkeley estate, which numbered 150 in 1572, though an economy drive brought the number down to a mere 80 by 1580. Heavy expenditure on clothes was another item, as evidenced by the £1000 and more in debts owed by the Earl of Arundel to various mercers and tailors. And not content with fabulous ostentation in life some peers were magnificent in death also. No doubt the £3000 spent on Leicester's funeral was exceptional, but other peers also were buried at a cost of £1000 and more—the Earl of Sussex for £1600 and the Earl of Pembroke for £2000. Not all noble estates could easily bear such charges.

The incomes of peers varied so greatly that it is dangerous to talk of an average, but probably most fell between £600 and £1500 in the first half of the century and between £2000 and £3000 towards its end. A favoured minister might do much better than this; Thomas Cromwell's income was nearly £8000 for only eight months in 1535–36, and Hertford's income was £4400 by 1547. But only a few were rewarded on this scale, and most grants to peers were quite small. As a group they certainly benefited from low taxation, their assessments for payment of subsidies become more and more ludicrous towards 1600. Burghley, worth perhaps £4000 from his lands alone, was returned in the lay subsidy assessments as having an income of only £133 right up to his death in 1598. This was some recompense for the considerable services rendered by the peerage, though it would not go far to meet the costs of those who served as ambassadors or military expeditions—these normally left the unhappy lord seriously out of pocket.

In view of their necessary and unnecessary expenses many peers got into debt. The size of an individual's debts is, however, a poor indication of the overall state of his finances. Most peers were relatively rich in land, but lacked ready cash, and to raise cash they had to borrow or mortgage.

Only those who could offer good security would be able to raise large loans, and thus only the richest could acquire large debts. Unless we have reason to believe that a peer's debts amounted to a large proportion of his capital the mere sum of them does not prove his poverty. The fact that he incurred debts at all does not necessarily indicate that he was in financial straits; it may mean only that he was temporarily short of ready money.

More cogent evidence of a decline of aristocratic fortunes is supplied in Professor Tawney's analysis of manors owned by them in the period 1540–1640. Whether the peers are defined as those families holding peerages throughout the period, or as those holding or requiring them at any time during it, his figures suggest a drop in the number of manors held. Though on the second method of calculation they owned as a group about the same total number in 1640 as in 1561. The figures are, however, open to serious criticism.

The sample chosen by Tawney, though containing over 2500 manors, is confined to only seven counties. Since peers and gentry alike often owned estates in several counties, such a restricted sample is no safe guide to the wealth of any individual; apparent gains and losses within these seven counties may well be balanced by others in counties outside the sample. A more basic objection is that the manor is not a satisfactory unit of measurement. It is not an economic, but a legal entity, and the size and wealth of manors might vary very widely indeed. It can be argued that a sample of 2500 is big enough to offset this difficulty, and that a rough average can be assumed. But we are peculiarly concerned with the manors that changed hands rather than the total numbers owned by peers and others, and it is therefore very important to know just which manors were disposed of, and how large and prosperous they were. A peer might increase his income by selling several small manors which were widely separated from the main bloc of his estates, and thus costly and difficult to administer. It would be misleading to reckon such a man as an example of aristocratic decline.

It is not clear, either, whether in fact peers lost ground by unbusinesslike estate-management. Again it is easy to find individual examples, the third Earl of Cumberland being a conspicuous one. In addition to the £100,000 or so that he lost on grandiose privateering expeditions, in themselves partly an attempt to make good former extravagances, he was an inefficient absentee landlord. It is true that his absenteeism, by attendance at court, helped him to grants of land and of the valuable monopoly of licences for the export of unfinished cloth (1602) and that this last was a major asset worth £2500 a year. It is also true that his inefficiency was partly due to the very weakness of his position; he could not drive hard bargains with his tenants. But the result was that he had to grant unprofitable long-term leases to his tenants, thus hindering his successors' efforts to make good the damage, and that after 1602 he resorted to considerable sales of land, thus reducing his successors' capital. When he died in 1605 the Clifford inheritance was far poorer than when he reached his majority in 1579, and this was partly due to bad estate-management.

On the other hand the Spencers of Althorp built up their wealth by efficient farming of their estates, aided by restraint in expenditure and well-planned marriages. By the early 17th century their income may have been as high as £8000, achieved without the help of lucrative offices or spectacular crown grants. They are a prime example of a family that achieved a peerage through sustained economic effort. The truth is that we can easily find examples of both provident and spendthrift peers, and it is dangerous to generalise for the whole class on the strength of either group. The same applies to the gentry. Within a single family the conduct of affairs changed from generation to generation, and the extravagance of one thriftless landlord could undo the patient work of many predecessors. No simple contrast between aristocratic improvidence and gentry efficiency will help to explain the fortunes of the two classes.

How far, and in what sense did the gentry gain either

economically or socially during the 16th century? The term "gentry" is, of course, extremely vague. The lack of a title sharply divided the upper gentry from the peerage, though we have to remember that the peerage was not an economic class and that a title of nobility did not make a peer richer than a knight. But it is not at all helpful, probably not even possible, to set a similar legal limit for the lesser gentry, and to insist on a grant of arms as the distinguishing mark of the class. Such a dividing line would be far too arbitrary and unreliable, even if we could pick our way through the maze of false claims to gentility. It would certainly not help us in a discussion of the gentry's economic situation. To contemporaries the gentry were no doubt those who were so reckoned by the people of their locality, but this is not a test that we can apply. Local standing was largely determined by wealth and a display of hospitality. But the connection was by no means automatic, and standards of wealth varied greatly from one part of the country to another. The yeomen whose income Thomas Wilson reckoned at £300 to £500 a year "and some twice and some thrice as much" would have ranked as wealthy gentlemen in the poorer areas of north-west England. In most cases we have no means of distinguishing between gentry and yeomanry, and the dividing lines were not perfectly clear even at the time. Of the former the most we can say is that they were a class of usually middling prosperity, who at the upper limit of income might be richer than the nobility, and at the lower merged imperceptibly into the yeomanry. Their social standing was likewise between the two, though here the upper limit at least was sharply defined. It is only with the utmost caution that we can pronounce on the fortunes of a class so vaguely delineated.

Figures presented by Tawney for his seven counties would suggest that middling landowners (i.e. those owning four manors or less) gained ground in the period 1561–1640, the proportion of manors owned by them rising from 57 to 64 per cent of the whole. This is not a very spectacular increase, and almost all of it occurred after 1601, not in the Tudor period. The holdings of large landowners apparently drop from 24 to 16½ per cent, but nearly all of this is accounted for by the sale of crown lands, not those of peers. Tawney's figures therefore do not support the idea that middling land-owners made enormous gains during the 16th century, nor that they did so at the expense of the aristocracy.

Among the substantial landowners and among those clearly regarded by their contemporaries as having gentry status it is easy to find examples of men rising and falling in wealth. This is true at any period of history for any reason-ably large class. Those who rise tend to catch the attention of the historian, while only the more spectacular failures arouse his interest and leave tangible evidence. Hence almost any history-book tells us that the most significant fact about the social history of England in any century of modern times is the Rise of the Middle Classes. It is unusual for any author to try to show that this rise was especially rapid during the period he is discussing, or to point out that while some men rose out of obscurity others quietly faded into it. For the 16th century there is not enough evidence to argue convin-cingly for the general or rapid rise of a middle or gentry class, however this be defined. Much more than a survey of manors in seven counties would be necessary. Nor have we enough instances of the rise and fall of individuals to generalize with any confidence as to what factors determined their respective fates. We can offer only some plausible suggestions.

It has been suggested that efficient estate-management brought wealth to the gentry (by contrast with the feckless aristocracy). Certainly profits could be made by engrossing, enclosure and conversion to pasture, and careful attention to one's estates might mean the difference between prosperity and indigence. But not all landowners were in a position to enclose and convert, and it was easier to lose a fortune by negligence than to build one by hard application. Large-scale improvements were difficult for those who lacked large capital to start with, and lesser landowners could not afford to employ the skilled administrative personnel required. Extensive credit was also necessary to the big farmer, and it was difficult to become a big farmer without it. Conditions thus worked against the landowner who hoped to make his fortune by efficient farming alone. Rack-renting of the tenantry was a likelier way to an increased income, but here the opportunities varied widely in different areas, and landlords faced with a numerous body of freeholders and well-secured copyholders could not resort to it. In general land-ownership conferred gentility and local prestige rather than opened a royal road to wealth.

It might be added here that the Dissolution of the Monasteries did not create a new class of wealthy gentry. The monastic lands were for the most part—as far as our present knowledge goes—sold at a fair market price, and the price was adjusted as the general level of prices rose later in the century. Real bargains were rare, and more likely in the case of urban rents and properties than land. Hence those who bought monastic properties had to have substantial capital to do so, and it was not normally possible to buy them for a song and make a fortune on the resale. Nor, since many of these properties were already efficiently farmed and strictly rented, was there often an opportunity to profit from the exploitation of hitherto undeveloped estates. The disposal of them by the crown enabled some established landowners to round off their possessions; it did not create new landed wealth where none had been before.

The holding of office under the crown was a quicker way to get rich. Though the official fees were often nominal there were rich pickings to be had on the side—in, for example, the Court of Wards—and since these came from the pockets of litigants and suitors the crown was able to economise on the salaries of its servants. Favoured servants and courtiers might also obtain valuable export licences and monopolies that could be disposed of to merchants and industrial promoters. It was this type of monopoly, given as a reward to a favourite rather than to foster a new invention, that came under heavy criticism towards the end of the century. Obviously not all royal servants were rewarded on the scale of Thomas Cromwell or William Cecil, but posts in the customs service were not ill-rewarded, and merely to be in personal favour with the monarch would produce a stream of presents from those who sought a patron to act as intermediary. It was worth considerable expenditure of money and effort to obtain office and a place in the sun.

The snag was that no one could be sure of success, and in the meanwhile expenditure was heavy. To attend regularly at court involved keeping a town residence. To appear before the monarch meant owning an imposing wardrobe; it would not do to come before Elizabeth I dowdily dressed. As fashions became more extravagant, so this expense constantly rose, and court attendance was undoubtedly more costly in 1603 than in 1485. To impress those seeking his patronage and good offices the courtier had to live in style and offer hospitality, and this added still further to his outlay. There was also a concealed cost. To live in London was to neglect one's estates, and only an exceptionally honest and efficient bailiff could compensate for the owner's prolonged absence. Thus the third Earl of Cumberland gained his valuable monopoly of the export of unfinished cloth, but left seriously depleted estates; his successor lost the monopoly, probably in large part through non-attendance at court, but was able to do something to arrest the decline of his lands. It was very difficult to assess the chances, and expensive to guess wrong.

Professor Trevor-Roper has rightly stressed the political and social division between the court and country gentry, the latter being those living demurely on their estates cut off from the fountain of patronage and favour. Whether office-holding had quite the economic significance that he attaches to it is a little more doubtful. Once again it is easy to quote examples of the successful few, but were they enough to alter the balance of wealth in the country? And though the ultimate gains might be great, the initial stake was not negligible. Trevor-Roper himself stresses the cost of the advanced

5

education that qualified a man for office, and the heavy expense of continued residence at court. All this outlay had the nature of a speculative investment, which was amply rewarded in the case of the successful, but represented a heavy loss to the unsuccessful. The former were tempted to recoup their expenses by exploiting their positions; the latter could only retire disappointed to their country estates. Whether on balance the pursuit of office was a gainful occupation is virtually impossible to say.

Fortunes could also be made in trade or the law. The scale of operations and the personal wealth of Tudor merchants rose throughout the century, though the evidence is rather fragmentary, and it is difficult to say how far their incomes kept ahead of rising prices. Already by the mid-century there are merchant wills suggesting personal fortunes of £6000, exclusive of lands, though wills rarely specify the exact extent of the testator's possessions. Numerous merchants bought the lands of the dissolved monasteries, several paying over £1000. The wealthiest merchant of the early Tudor period, Richard Gresham, paid over £11,000 for the abbey of Fountains, and the annual value of his lands at his death was said to be £800. Another early Tudor merchant, William Hollies, left lands worth £365 a year. Others owned numerous manors scattered in many counties, like Rowland Heyward with his eighteen country manors and considerable properties in London also. Such figures are not spectacular when measured against the wide estates of the wealthier peers and landed gentry, but it must be remembered that such properties were built up from almost nothing within a single lifetime, and therefore represent a rapid accumulation of wealth. If Thomas Gresham's profits of nearly 15 per cent per year were at all typical, a merchant could clearly expect to make money faster than any farmer; five per cent was still considered a fair return on land, though this conventional figure may have been an underestimate. The fact that so many merchants bought estates is evidence that they sought a safe investment and social respectability rather than further profit; after 1571 they could make ten per cent a year by money-lending with much less trouble to themselves.

Once again, however, we have to consider the failures as well as the successes. Thomas Gresham weathered the commercial crisis of 1551 by pulling out of active trade. Others were less far-sighted and were ruined. Throughout the century we hear of at least a small number of merchants who went bankrupt or died in poverty. Such, for example, was Avery Rawson, at one time a prosperous Stapler and Mercer, who in 1515 was granted £20 by the Mercers since he had "lately sustained many great losses, whereby he is grown much in poverty and necessity." This help did him little good, and five years later he was reported to have "deceitfully, rebukefully and shamefully withdrawn himself from this City of London." At least two other Mercers of the early 16th century absconded from London to avoid meeting their creditors. Other merchants, so far as we can judge from the customs accounts, continued year after year without greatly expanding their business. Our evidence tends to focus attention on the wealthy few, the men who feature in the great trading companies and who left vast charitable benefactions in their wills. Others, who have left no such mark on official records and who founded no great country estates, slip quietly out of view.

The same applies to another lucrative calling, that of the law. The Tudor age was intensely litigious, and there was no lack of business for lawyers. Admissions at the four Inns of Court averaged about forty a year at the beginning and over two hundred at the end of the century. Some lawyers became wealthy men and left substantial estates to their heirs. But not all. Justices like Robert Brudenell and Chancellors like Nicholas Bacon founded great properties, and the Serjeants with their monopoly of pleading civil cases in the Court of Common Pleas could also do well for themselves. A training in law was also frequently a prelude to an official career, and what is distinctive about the Tudor "new men" is this professional education rather than their social origins. More and Cromwell were both trained lawyers, as were eighteen out of twenty-one Speakers of the Commons up to 1558. But only a few rose to such eminence, and even if we discount some three-quarters of the young gentlemen who thronged the Inns of Court in the 1570's as though attending a finishing school or "third university", there were many barristers and attorneys who depended on their quite modest fees and achieved no more than a modest success. The prospects of a young lawyer might be without limit, but room at the top was restricted. Lavish contemporary abuse of their greed and wealth does grave injustice to most of the profession.

It may well be true that the gentry class found its new recruits chiefly among the officials, the merchants and the lawyers. It was certainly possible for them to make money and a reputation more rapidly than any yeoman patiently building up his estates. All three groups could ride the wave of inflation more easily than the landowner faced with strongly entrenched tenants and established customs. Arrived on his new estate the wealthy Londoner might well find it easier to establish his position than did the local rich yeoman, who was barred by his neighbours' social conservatism from gaining recognition as a gentleman. But the numbers of these new rich can never have been very great, and since moreover some of them sprang from landed families in the first place their arrival cannot have tilted the balance of landed wealth very far.

Below the gentry in the scale of landowners stood the yeomen, another class whose upper and lower limits are impossible to determine precisely. Contemporaries viewed them in a somewhat ambivalent way. On the one hand they were seen as the backbone of the nation, or, as Sir Thomas Smith put it, "the liver-veins of the Commonwealth, yielding both good juice and nourishment to all other parts thereof." As a group they are praised by nearly every Elizabethan writer who discusses the social structure of his age, especially when the English class system is being compared with others abroad. They are distinguished by their industry, frugality, patriotism and solid worth. On the other hand premature claims to gentility on their part aroused the derision of the dramatists:

> Come, off with this trash,
> Your bought Gentility, that sits on thee
> Like Peacock's feathers cock't upon a Raven.

And the moralist Crowley admonished the yeoman in 1550:

> Have mind, therefore, thyself to hold
> Within the bounds of thy degree
> And then thou mayest ever be bold
> That God thy Lord will prosper thee.

But it was freely admitted that the yeoman's son might better himself—though not too rapidly and preferably not within the locality of his birth. Intermarriage between gentry and yeoman families was common, and social relations often friendly and intimate. The ambitious yeoman could put his son to study the law or another of the liberal professions and hope that he might thus raise his family's social standing. William Harrison describes the process in a much-quoted passage in his *Description of England*:

Gentlemen. . . . do take their beginning in England, after this manner in our times. Whosoever studieth the laws of the realm, whoso abideth in the university . . . or professeth physic and the liberal sciences, or beside his service in the room of a captain in the wars, (or good counsel given at home, whereby his commonwealth is benefited) can live without manual labour, and thereto is able and will bear the port, charge, and countenance of a gentleman, he shall (for money have a coat and arms bestowed upon him by heralds who in the charter of the same do of custom pretend antiquity and service) and thereunto being made so good cheap, be called master, which is the title that men give to esquires and gentlemen.

Established gentlemen might sometimes resent the competition of such yeomen's sons seeking to climb the social ladder, but such resentment does not seem to have been intense or widespread, and was never formalised in legislation. The expense of higher education or the premiums charged by merchants taking on yeoman-born apprentices might be an economic deterrent, but there were no legal checks to advancement.

Here we are concerned with those yeomen who were content with, even proud of their status, and did not aspire to rise into the ranks of the gentry. There is no doubt that such men existed and would have sincerely echoed the playwrite's sentiment:

> Let Gentlemen go gallant, what care I,
> I was a yeoman born, and so I'll die.

Pride apart, there were some material advantages in remaining a mere yeoman. He was not expected to entertain on the same scale as his gentry neighbours. Though he might play his part in local government as sheriff's bailiff or in some similar capacity, the more costly honorary posts did not fall to him. His military obligations were also lighter. He was unlikely to be tempted to compete for office or prestige at court. Relatively free from social and official obligations he could husband his resources and concentrate on the management of his estates.

Yeomen were certainly avid purchasers of land, often in substantial amounts. An analysis of some 4000 transactions by them between 1570 and 1640 shows purchases ranging up to £2100, and though 59 per cent of these were for less than £100, as many as 441 (14 per cent) ranged between £200 and £500, while 262 (8 per cent) were above £500. Where purchase was impossible they bought long leases that were tantamount to purchase—in some fanciful cases for as long as 5000 or 10,000 years. Once in effective possession the new owner was able to take advantage of the general increase in rents and so recoup his outlay, though often he himself might be paying greatly enhanced rents for other parts of his estates. Because most transactions by yeomen were on a relatively modest scale they may be quite inadequately represented in Tawney's table, dealing only in manors. The wealthy Lincolnshire yeoman Robert Phillips bought the manor of Wishington for £1006 in 1585, but this was no doubt an unusual case and Phillips was being described as a gentleman by 1603. Most of his fellows bought their land in substantial but less conspicuous parcels, and the cumulative effect of these purchases is hard to assess.

Yeomen were sometimes classed by contemporaries with the more ruthless and avaricious enclosing gentry. This is hardly surprising when wealthy yeomen were economically indistinguishable from the lesser gentry. But though it is certainly possible to find cases of encroachment on commons, eviction and rack-renting fairly laid to their charge, they were not usually among the more serious offenders. Their enclosures were usually on a small scale, often by agreement rather than by coercion, and since they were often made for tillage rather than pasture escaped the censure of contemporary opponents of depopulation.

The estates and incomes of yeomen varied so widely that it is difficult to generalise usefully about them. Mildred Campbell suggests that their estates may have ranged from 25 to 200 acres in predominantly arable areas and as high as 500 or 600 acres in grazing regions. Incomes varied not only with the size but also the richness of the lands. Contemporary remarks about yeoman wealth were relative, and the term "wealthy" means different things in different counties. Thomas Wilson in 1600 estimated that there were some 10,000 wealthy yeomen in England, of whom some had incomes of £300 to £500. These probably lived mainly in East Anglia and south-eastern England, since such incomes would have qualified their possessors as gentlemen of great rank in Devon or Cornwall, where £40 to £100 was considered by one writer to be normal for a yeoman. Wilson also estimated that there were some 60,000 less wealthy yeomen in the England of his day, and it seems likely that the poorer of these may well have had as little as £40 a year, living barely above the level of the more prosperous husbandman.

Inventories of 2172 yeomen in three counties between 1556 and 1650 show an average personal estate of £160, but a random sample of four of them shows a range from £75 to £861, while a Suffolk inventory of 1583 shows a total personal estate of only £27. The average is thus only a very rough guide.

The descriptions of Wilson and Harrison are probably over-enthusiastic and exaggerate the prosperity of the yeoman class. Once again we are in danger of paying too much attention to its successful members only. Against those who prospered and rose into the gentry must be set the less well-documented cases of those who saw a progressive diminution of their estates through bad management or pressure of outside circumstances, or who suffered catastrophic loss through the vagaries of the harvest or the diseases that attacked their flocks. Such men would in time fade into the ranks of the husbandmen and peasants, even if for a time local courtesy still accorded them the title of yeomen. There is no way of assessing the gains and losses of the group as a whole. Since contemporary opinion was so emphatic that the yeomen were a prosperous and solid class it may be that the gains outweighed the losses, but the 16th century was not an age of statistical precision. It can reasonably be suggested the general rise in food prices and rents, running ahead of rising wages for both urban and agricultural labour, favoured the substantial farmer who held most of his estates in freehold or on a long lease. Given his reasonable share of good fortune, the yeoman could expect to prosper. He could not hope for the windfalls of court office or a monopoly, nor for the high profits of the successful merchant. But he was spared the distractions of costly social life and the burden of unpaid office. The time and effort that a farmer devoted to his estates was probably the most important single factor determining his success or failure. Thus this freedom to concentrate on his business was probably just as important as the general economic climate in aiding the prosperity of the Tudor yeoman. Not until he rose into the gentry class would

he experience its temptations or find that his expenses ran
ahead of his income.

The position of the small freeholder was similar to that of
the yeoman. In an active land-market the most prosperous
peasants were just as anxious as their betters to enlarge and
consolidate their holdings, and the manorial rolls of, say,
East Anglia, are filled with their modest transactions. In
the second half of the century they were responsible for
nearly one-fifth of the enclosures in Leicestershire. Their
wills and inventories show the same progression, on a more
modest scale, towards greater prosperity and comfort. Once
again conditions favoured the industrious and thrifty. Those
who sold their produce for the market were borne up by the
rising tide of prices; those who produced mainly for their
own subsistence were at least protected against the worst
effects of inflation.

Of the rural classes only those with insecure tenure, copyholders and tenants at will, were truly vulnerable to the indirect effects of rising prices. Just how liable they were to
eviction and dispossession has been shown in another chapter. In so far as their misfortunes were due to the efforts of
the landlords to keep pace with rising prices they might be
considered the victims of the price revolution. But since at
least some landlords raised rents and fines above the level of
current prices, and since many enclosures had taken place
before 1510, the price revolution was but one factor among
many. The direct victims were the agricultural labourer
without land of his own—a small class—and the urban
worker dependent on wages.

The Brown/Hopkins price index is accompanied by one
that shows the equivalent wage-rate of a building craftsman
in southern England, i.e. the purchasing-power of his wages
in relation to the rising price of consumables. This would
suggest a catastrophic drop in the urban worker's real wages,
since it rarely rises above 60 in the second half of the century
and rarely above 40 from 1595 to 1619; in the crisis year
1597 it drops as low as 29. It seems hardly possible that such
5*

a drop can have taken place without far greater outcry than we have record of. To accept the figures at their face-value would mean that urban workers were dying of starvation in thousands at the end of the 16th century and in the early Stuart period. Some factors have surely been left out of account.

It is not necessary to labour the point that wage-rates are not the same as earnings, though this of course cuts two ways; the building labourer may have earned more than his wage-rate suggests in times of full employment and less at others. He may also have received a supplement to his wages in the form of meals and accommodation on the job, and such payments in kind would cushion him against inflation. More important still, the urban labourer of the 16th century was not as fully urbanised as his 20th century successor, and would often have a plot of land or at least a garden on which he could cultivate his own food. In these various ways his harsh lot was somewhat mitigated.

But with this said it remains true that the urban worker did suffer a substantial fall in his standard of living, and that this was largely due to rising prices. Whereas in Spain and the Netherlands wages rose at roughly the same rate as food-prices, though with a short time-lag before each re-adjustment, in England and France they trailed a long way behind. Tudor workers lacked trade unions and political representatives to plead their case effectively, and the legislation of 1563 was designed to hold wages down rather than force them up. Cheap labour may have aided the prosperity of industrial employers in Elizabeth's reign. It meant real hunger and hardship for a substantial number of the working population.

The impact of the so-called price-revolution thus varied from class to class and from one occupational group to another. It did not necessarily have any serious effect on those who made their living by direct exploitation of the soil, since the price of food tended always to rise more than that of other consumables. For this group, and it comprised the overwhelming majority of the Tudor population, wealth or poverty depended on individual and personal circumstances. For those who depended on relatively fixed incomes that they were powerless to change the rise in prices inevitably brought hardship and a declining standard of living. This group included both landlords who lived on rents rather than farming and labourers mainly dependent on wages. To a third, much smaller group, who were able and willing to exploit a changing situation, the price-rise brought great opportunities. Among these were businesslike and ruthless landlords, lawyers benefiting from an active land-market, and merchants with a keen eye to commercial opportunity. The ultimate balance of gains and losses is, as usual in this period, impossible to assess.

Did the price-rise, then, have no great effect on the social structure of Tudor England? The answer is probably that its impact has been exaggerated in the past. As at all periods of English history some men were ascending and others descending the economic and social ladder. In some cases this movement was no doubt speeded up by inflation. But inflation did not create a new class of wealthy men, nor of itself bring about a significant shift in the balance of political power. The events of the 17th century showed that such a shift had indeed taken place, but it can only in small part be attributed to the price-rise or the redistribution of church property. More important factors in all probability were the decline of the nobility's military influence and the very gradual substitution of the more nebulous patron-client relationship in place of the overlord-tenant connection. The gradual emergence of an educated laity and a centralised bureaucracy worked in the same direction. Government ceased to be dependent on the aristocracy when it neither feared them for their military resources nor needed them as political advisers.

The contemporary attitude to social change was not altogether clear-cut, and there was something of a divorce between theory and practice. Writers and moralists still clung to the idea of an ordered hierarchy of society, in which each man held a clearly allotted "degree" within a divinely ordered system. In principle it was presumptuous to aspire to a higher degree, and general failure to observe due order and degree could only be the prelude to social anarchy. The classical, much-quoted expression of this view is Ulysses' speech in *Troilus and Cressida*:

> O, when degree is shak'd,
> Which is the ladder to all high designs,
> The enterprise is sick. How could communities,
> Degrees in schools, and brotherhoods in cities,
> Peaceful commerce from dividable shores,
> The primogenitive and due of birth,
> Prerogative of age, crowns, sceptres, laurels,
> But by degree, stand in authentic place?
> Take but degree away, untune that string,
> And, hark, what discord follows.

Social conservatism and the intense Tudor dread of civil war here find eloquent expression. But though crabbed peers might sneer at the newest members of their order, and though moralists might reprove the pretensions of the gentleman arriviste, society was in practice more tolerant than the literature of the age would suggest. The acquisition of wealth led to quite speedy social recognition, in the second generation if not the first, though preferably the wealth had to be invested in land. Intermarriage between the children of peers and gentry, or gentry and yeomen, was a commonplace event; a rich dowry fully compensated for any suggestion of mésalliance. Personal distinction, especially in war or politics, would offset lowly birth, though success in either field would probably lead to the acquisition of property sufficient to ensure respect on its own account. Thus though Tudor society was undoubtedly more class-conscious than our own, an able man could climb without meeting serious obstacles, and wealth acquired respectability within a generation. After all, not many Tudor peers could genuinely claim ancient noble descent, and the De la Pole's, whose nearness to the throne cost them so heavily under Henry VIII, owed their start in the world to a 14th century wool-merchant.

It has often been asked if the greater opportunities of the 16th century led to a more ruthless and unscrupulous attitude in economic and social life. Were Tudor landlords more harsh, Tudor merchants more avaricious and usurious than their medieval forebears? Was this change, if change there were, associated with the Protestant faith? If Capitalism is defined as the rational pursuit of profit, without undue regard for social consequences, was there any causal relation between Capitalism and the rise of Protestantism?

The alleged change of attitude may well be an optical illusion. The literature of social complaint is much more abundant for the Tudor period than for earlier times. This is true not only of deliberate propaganda, the sermons and pamphlets that were more widely disseminated at the time and have survived in greater numbers down to our own day owing to the use of printing. It is true also of legal records. Some of these become more copious in the 16th century, like the records of the Court of Chancery; in some cases the courts themselves were substantially new creations, such as Star Chamber and the Court of Requests. For the first time, therefore, we have plenty of evidence of misdeeds of all kinds, and the statements of them are highly rhetorical and usually entirely one-sided. And since social propagandists write mainly of what is amiss, and since court records deal exclusively with what is allegedly amiss, it is easy to conclude that Tudor England was struck by an unprecedented crime-wave and that all manner of malpractices sprang into being for the first time. This is not really very probable. It is much more likely that the evidence rather than the misbehaviour is new, and that we have no special reason to think ill of Tudor landowners and businessmen.

It may also be doubted whether the opportunities were so unprecedented or the capitalistic spirit so new or pronounced. The 14th century had seen great fortunes made and lost in the wool trade, and the lucrative monopoly of the Merchant Adventurers was not wholly new. The cloth industry had had its great names in the 15th century, and the Paycocks of Coggeshall preceded the Springs of Lavenham and the Winchcombes of Newbury. Italian merchant-banking firms of the 15th century exceeded in scale and sophistication of business technique any Tudor business house. By the more advanced contemporary standards 16th century London merchants were not fully rational and calculating in their pursuit of gain.

Many historians are very sceptical, too, of the allegedly corrupting influence of Protestant business ethics. It has been pointed out that the Reformers were only to a small extent concerned with the world of business, and that their occasional pronouncements on commercial questions—notably usury—have been torn from a wider context and given a quite false and exaggerated emphasis. Calvin in particular has suffered from this arbitrary treatment, and on the strength of a few pages among the many thousands of his writings has been presented as the apostle of a new ethic consciously designed for hard-headed businessmen. In fact he is overwhelmingly concerned with the duty to God owed by all Christian men, and only very occasionally touches on the particular problems of the business community. Furthermore the pronouncements of the leading Reformers, when they did deal with commercial topics, were uniformly conservative in their emphasis and upheld the traditional duties of the Christian to his neighbour. They did not encourage or condone the uncontrolled pursuit of profit, still less the doctrine that the acquisition of great wealth was a sign of divine favour. Some self-satisfied merchants in Protestant countries may indeed have come to believe that riches were the reward of Godliness, but this attitude was characteristic of the 17th century rather than the 16th, and could find no encouragement in the writings of John Calvin. There was perhaps in the event some connection between Calvinism and business success. Though both Catholic and

Calvinist churches preached a doctrine of hard work and good stewardship, the Calvinists were in practice more successful in instilling the virtues of thrift and industry into their disciples. These virtues were undoubtedly good for business, and the merchants of London, Amsterdam and La Rochelle prospered accordingly. But this was a triumph for effective moral education and not the victory of a novel doctrine. It may well be that in the 17th century the successful businessman pursued his profits more single-mindedly and less charitably. But in so far as this happened it affected Catholic and Protestant alike, and the moralists of both camps fought hard against the new trend. Protestantism in Tudor England did not foster a secular or capitalistic spirit.

Recent scholarship suggests that, so far from deserting the good example of their forefathers, the most successful businessmen of the age—the London merchant community —took the lead in fostering social works and charitable foundations. Professor W. K. Jordan's *Philanthropy in England, 1480–1660* produces massive evidence for this view. His general claim that charitable donations saw a prodigious increase during this period is not acceptable, since he calmly ignores the factor of inflation. His analysis of charitable bequests by social class and geographical area remains valid, however, for comparative purposes, and his discussion of the changing direction of these bequests is interesting and important.

Jordan classifies 438 out of 2677 London merchants as "greater merchants", and estimates that they constitute one-sixth of the London merchant community and about 6 per cent of his London benefactors. Their charitable bequests in the period 1480–1660 totalled £907,000, nearly half of the London total, and perhaps 16 per cent of the entire country. Their bequests average more than £2000. This represents a very impressive performance, not only by the greater merchants as individuals, but even more as a group. Equally impressive is the care and foresight bestowed in the giving.

Random distributions of alms to the poor were rare. Some 93 per cent of the money given for poor-relief was in the form of well-organised trusts, which stood the test of time amazingly well. Moreover, by contrast with the donors of other cities and counties (such as Bristol) the London merchants gave extensively to charities all over the country. This was especially marked in the field of education, where the £178,000 left by the greater London merchants for the foundation of grammar-schools represented 40 per cent of all such donations in the ten counties covered by Jordan's study. Few individuals could endow foundations on the scale of St. John's College, Oxford (Thomas White) or Gresham's college in London, which but for the indifference of the 18th century might have been the nucleus of London University. But their collective contribution to education was immense, and more than compensated for the (often exaggerated) damage done by Edward VI in the destruction of chantry schools.

The contribution of the lesser merchants of London was far more modest—their bequests averaged only £71. But on a reduced scale they showed the same concern as their betters for the relief of the poor and for charitable institutions like the London hospitals. Their concern with education was less intense; they left only some 12 per cent of their bequests to schools and universities, but this may be because not many could leave enough to endow a school of any size. They showed even less concern for religion than the wealthier merchants, leaving a bare 3 per cent of their money for religious purposes in the period 1561–1600. For both groups, of course, the dissolution of the monasteries and chantries brought to an end the most popular forms of religious benefaction, and some redistribution of funds was inevitable. But the lesser merchants did not show the same zeal even for the foundation of Puritan lectureships that marked some of the rich men. Latimer would, no doubt, have been grieved by this, but the London merchant class did not in fact illustrate his famous stricture that "charity waxeth cold." Their charitable giving was generous by any standards, and it certainly cannot be said that business success in Tudor England went along with callous unconcern for one's neighbour. It is unnecessarily cynical to attribute this generosity to deathbed repentance and a belated recognition of duty undone. And even on this low view of Tudor merchant morality, it can still be said that this class did more than others to make good its shortcomings.

The 16th century thus saw an unprecedented rise in prices, caused, we may tentatively suggest, by pressure of population on limited food-supplies and accelerated by debasement, government expenditure and easier credit facilities. Spanish silver may have played its part in the later decades of the century, but that is difficult to assess or demonstrate. This price-rise speeded up change in a society where change was accepted in fact if not in principle. Those who drew their living from the soil were often in a position to take advantage of the especially rapid increase in food-prices, though some might be prevented by legal contract or established convention. For those not so bound success was determined by business acumen and industry, and readiness to move with the times. A substantial number of gentry and yeomen manifestly prospered, though we must remember that many failures pass unrecorded. The victims, apart from the lazy or inefficient, were the peasants without security of tenure and the Church—and the losses of the latter were due to government action rather than the price-revolution. Outside the agrarian classes there were opportunities for some to make fortunes in trade, the law, or government posts and pensions; there were equally opportunities for unrequited expenditure and bankruptcy. The worst-hit were those furthest removed from the land and most dependent on wages. The urban labourer undoubtedly suffered a severe fall in his standard of living, if not quite as catastrophic as has been suggested. But he, like the dispossessed peasant, could hope for at least some relief from the class that showed most business skill and success in the Tudor period, the greater London merchants. Neither Protestantism nor Capitalism turned the good business man into a bad neighbour. He showed, on the contrary, more charitable concern for the unfortunate than did any other group. He would no doubt have echoed (though in Protestant terms) a favourite phrase of the Italian expert on double-entry bookkeeping, Luca Pacioli: *Nec caritas opes, nec missa minuit iter*. "Charity is not a waste of money, nor Mass a waste of time."

V

THE RÔLE OF GOVERNMENT

THERE IS NO DOUBT that the sixteenth century saw much more government intervention in economic and social life. Many of the "stacks of statutes" loaded on the shoulders of the Justices of the Peace dealt with matters such as the enforcement of regular apprenticeship, the regulation of wages, and the administration of poor relief. Frequent proclamations reinforced these statutes, or prescribed for immediate ills such as famine or the disruption of the monetary system. The intention and significance of all this legislation is, however, very debatable. Did any Tudor government have an economic or social policy worthy of the name? Or does this activity represent only a series of more or less happy improvisations? Was Tudor legislation effective in practice, or did most of the statutes and proclamations remain dead letters? On these questions historians have been, and still are, sharply divided.

Some 250 statutes of the Tudor period deal directly with economic matters, and analysis of them gives us an indication of those problems that the Tudors and their subjects held to be most important. Not a wholly satisfactory indication, it must be admitted, since some statutes reflect particu-

lar vested interests, whilst others are so brief and trivial that
their mere number is no true guide to the importance of the
topics dealt with. But the evidence of the statute book can
be supplemented by that of Tudor proclamations, incom-
plete as our list of these unfortunately is. A number of major
problems were dealt with by proclamation rather than by
statute—emergency measures to deal with food shortages,
for example, or prerogative matters such as regulation of the
currency. Licences and patents also give some indication of
government direction of the economy—or at least of the
way in which government measures were modified when
they came to be put into practice.

Acts to regulate industry and maintain standards of production make up much the largest group. As might be expected, the cloth industry has pride of place, and no fewer
than 34 acts deal with the old-established woollen manufacture and a further ten with the declining worsted industry
of Norwich and its hinterland. There was nothing new in
this. The length and breadth of broadcloths and kerseys had
been regulated long before the Tudors came to the throne,
the most recent act in the series being that of 1483. The aul-
nagers in every county had long had the task of examining
cloths and affixing leaden seals to certify their measurements. Tudor statutes merely extended this policy, prescribing in greater detail and for kinds of cloth hitherto un-
specified. The most elaborate act of the series was that of
1552, which not only laid down the official length and
breadth for 23 varieties of woollen, but also for the first
time specified standard weights as well: Worcester broadcloths, for example, were henceforth to be 23–25 yards in
length, $1\frac{3}{4}$ yards in breadth, and were to weigh at least 60
pounds. Later statutes either supplemented this one, or
allowed special exemptions for local branches of the industry
which found strict compliance unduly onerous.

The main beneficiaries of this legislation were probably
the merchants, who clearly had an interest in having supplies of standardised products on whose quality they could

rely. At least some merchants exported their cloths without any very rigorous inspection, and had subsequently to meet the complaints and demands for rebates of their Antwerp customers. The act of 1552 was the direct outcome of the commercial crisis or the previous year, which the Merchant Adventurers had blamed on the shoddiness of the clothiers' wares.

On the other hand, a series of acts which forbade the export of undyed and unfinished cloth above a certain value was certainly not to the Adventurers' liking, and was clearly intended to benefit the native cloth-finishing industry. The limit for unfinished cloths was fixed at £2 in 1487, and raised by stages to £4 in 1536 (when the great majority of broadcloths undoubtedly cost less than this). Individuals, however, were granted licences allowing them to export unfinished cloths below the specified price. In 1566 a new act was passed, insisting that such licences should contain a clause enforcing the export of one finished cloth for every nine unfinished ones. The Adventurers consistently opposed these restrictions on the grounds that they could find no ready sale for finished cloth in Germany or the Netherlands, countries whose cloth-finishing industries were more advanced than England's. In the event they did largely escape the consequences of the statutes; they were able to continue the export of unfinished cloth, leaving the handling of finished cloth to foreign merchants and other English trading companies.

It is difficult to say how far either series of acts was effective. The frequent re-enactment of those laying down the official measurements of cloth in itself suggests partial failure. The 1566 act more or less admitted the ineffectiveness of previous legislation on the export of unfinished cloth. Crown and parliament found it hard to reconcile the divergent wishes of merchant and clothier in the one case, of merchant and clothfinisher in the other. But probably the 1552 act contributed something to the continued high reputation of English broadcloth abroad down till the end of the century, and that of 1566 guaranteed the London clothworkers a livelihood without too much impeding the traffic of the Merchant Adventurers.

The ten acts that related to the worsted industry were intended not so much to maintain standards in an important branch of the export trade—worsteds were far from being that—as to arrest the decline of a once prosperous area, and to guarantee the local industry its share of the necessary raw material. They belong therefore with other local acts designed to protect the interests of particular cities or areas, rather than with the other statutes regulating the textile trade and industry. Essentially conservative in character, it is unlikely that they did much to arrest the decline; Norwich, along with Ipswich and Colchester, owed its renewed prosperity in Elizabeth's reign to alien immigrants and the "new draperies" rather than to the wise provision of crown or parliament.

Other industrial statutes aimed to protect the domestic rather than the foreign consumer. Some such acts imposed specified standards of production or banned certain current malpractices, as for example those for the crafts of upholstering (1495), pin-making (1543), linen (1559) and wax-making (1581). Others tried to secure that only qualified craftsmen practised particular occupations, an attempt that sometimes involved drawing lines of demarcation between two or more crafts within a broad field. The frequency of legislation for the leather industry was partly due to the difficulty of prescribing for two major branches of a single industry—the workers in tanned and white leather—whose techniques were substantially different. That there were no less than fifteen acts in all reminds us, too, that the industry was one of major importance and gave employment to many workers; this has too often been overlooked both by contemporaries, hypnotised by the splendours of the cloth trade, and by later historians, fascinated by the beginnings of the iron and coal industries. Needless to say, some of these acts were inspired by the selfish interests of groups anxious to preserve a valuable monopoly. Nevertheless, these groups had to convince crown and parliament that they had a valid case, and the preambles alleging the need to maintain good craftsmanship cannot be altogether brushed aside. Strict implementation of the acts was no doubt impossible without the co-operation of the gilds, but both official and popular opinion demanded worthy standards.

The insufficiency of existing legislation of this kind was recognised by the time of Elizabeth I's accession, as was the need for a more general statute to cover the major crafts as a whole. To generalise the rule of a seven-year apprenticeship in industry was one result of the great Act of Apprentices of 1563, an act which sought also to deal with the problems of wage-inflation and vagrancy. Professor Bindoff has suggested that this was not part of the crown's original intention, but that Cecil and his advisors aimed only to restrict wage increases more effectively and to provide for compulsory labour on the land. The government bill was substantially amended in the commons, and its final form was much more far-reaching than the first draft. It not only provided for regular wage-assessments by the J.P.'s and for compulsory apprenticeship on the land for unattached youths; it also established a detailed list of property qualifications that barred the sons of the very poor from admission to any gild, extended compulsory apprenticeship to the urban crafts, and made the seven-year term of apprenticeship universal. At the same time, so as to prevent the apprenticeship system being used simply as a source of cheap labour, masters were limited in the number of apprentices they might employ along with hired journeymen. But though the final statute was more far-reaching than the original government bill, it was not a revolutionary document. Gilds and companies had long charged premiums to their apprentices, and in the wealthier companies these were set so high that they excluded all but the sons of the well-to-do. The 1563 scale of property qualifications made no striking innovation, therefore, and was in any case set so low that only the sons of husbandmen and labourers were likely to be excluded from the crafts. The seven-year period was already widely established, in London and elsewhere, and the act only made a common practice universal. The element of compulsion in the towns was something of a novelty, but there can have been few young men who deliberately remained unapprenticed in towns where work was to be found, and unemployment or underemployment was a more serious problem than wilful idleness. The act was restrictive in that it confined industrial activity more rigidly than before within the limits of the gild system. On the other hand it affected only crafts already established in 1563; those that sprang up after that date—notably those connected with mining and metallurgy—could develop in relative freedom. It is not very likely that the commons in 1563 deliberately intended this result, and what has sometimes been taken as their liberalism was more probably mere lack of imagination and foresight.

The effectiveness of the act is, as usual, hard to assess. Evidence of the enforcement of most of its clauses is scanty, and what there is does not suggest very rigorous implementation. The enforcement of the apprenticeship clauses has been studied in great detail, on the other hand, and the author's conclusion runs as follows: "It [the seven-year term] was neglected by central and local government, with rare exceptions, throughout the eighty years before the Civil War, and the majority of prosecutions by all but professional informers were apparently ineffective; while the latter imposed compositions equivalent to a burdensome but presumably not ruinous tax." But since apprenticeship was a universally accepted institution, and the seven-year term already coming into effect voluntarily, the absence of many successful prosecutions under the act of 1563 does not mean its total failure, though its application was probably lax in times of trade expansion. It did provide a uniform standard, and, it has been suggested, may even have helped to secure free entry into occupations otherwise hedged about by private privilege. Once again, perhaps, the act proved to be more liberal than its framers intended.

It was more difficult to legislate for moral standards than for technical ones. Church and state were at one in condemning the charging of interest on loans and the striking of usurious bargains. They continued to uphold the idea that there was a "just" price for both labour and goods, and that there was something iniquitous in high profits and swollen wages. This view owed a great deal to the long period of price stability that had preceded the Tudor age, even though the labour shortage after the Black Death had produced pressure for higher wages. It was much more difficult to maintain in a period of rapid inflation, especially when the causes of the inflation were imperfectly understood and each section of society blamed the others for bringing it about. (*The Discourse of the Common Weal* gives an eloquent example of this mutual recrimination.) Other factors also worked to weaken traditional concepts. Newly developed trades and advancing commercial technique made possible the amassing of rapid fortunes by the few, and sophisticated evasions of long-established bans. The ban on interest-charges was modified by the teaching of one of the new churches. Far too much has been made of Calvin's authorisation of usury by some of his critics, and the very heavy qualifications with which he surrounded it are usually forgotten. The relaxation in traditional teaching that he permitted was in fact very slight, and governments that officially condemned the taking of interest had been compelled to pay it to their creditors before Calvin ever wrote. Nonetheless, the fact that a church leader officially sanctioned the taking of interest, even under rigid restrictions, made it that much harder to maintain the unconditional veto. And perhaps some encouragement was given to the "takers of advantages".

Legislation against usury (in the narrower sense of the word) followed a wavering course. Two acts of 1487 attempted to curb the evil by legislating against the giving of fraudulent gifts, the practice of "dry exchange", and the malpractices of unlicensed money-exchangers, and a further act was passed in 1495. A major reversal came in 1545, when for the first time it became legal to charge interest of up to ten per cent on straight loans. The accounts of Thomas Gresham during the years 1546–51 show that merchants promptly availed themselves of the opportunity. But in 1552 this act was repealed, the preamble to the new act complaining of the "great and open usury daily used and practised", contrary to the intention of the 1545 act. In 1571, however, the ban was lifted once again and interest up to ten per cent allowed once more. This may conceivably represent the victory of a more acquisitive society over medieval ideas of justice and charity. It was not, however, a victory for Calvinism; it was the doctrinally orthodox Henry VIII who first relaxed the old ban at a time of conservative reaction, and Northumberland and his reforming government that reimposed it in the year of the second Edwardian prayer book.

A similar series of acts continued medieval attempts to curb the misdemeanours of forestallers, engrossers and regraters. The offence of the first two was that they "cornered" supplies of scarce goods (including foodstuffs) before they reached the market, and then forced up prices by exploiting a temporary local monopoly; the regraters bought and sold goods within a market, and raised prices by taking a profit for services of no apparent use to anyone. How far they were really a menace to Tudor markets, and how far they merely shared with enclosing landlords the rôle of universal scapegoat, is difficult to say. Acts such as that of 1552 (which incidentally gave formal definitions of the offences) suggest that they were an abiding nuisance. It is unlikely, on the other hand, that their sinister influence had much to do with the dearth of grain in the 1590's, though proclamations repeatedly declare them to be the chief culprits. Perhaps some abuses were checked by the fines and prison sentences threatened, but it is difficult not to suspect that the Tudors had an exaggerated suspicion of even the useful middleman in trade.

It might be suggested that not all acts aimed at the middleman were meant solely to bring down prices for the ordinary consumer. An act of 1552, limiting the purchase of wool to Staplers and cloth manufacturers, so eliminating the wool-brogger as an intermediary, served the purposes of two powerful vested interests more than the general public. Of the cloth manufacturers it benefited mainly the wealthy ones, those who operated on a large scale and bought their raw material in bulk. Lesser clothiers, who could not afford long journeys to buy their modest supplies, depended on the wool-broggers to keep them going; the new act was not at all to their advantage. Nor in the long run did it prove to the advantage of the Staplers, who had hoped to reduce competition in the buying of wool on the home market. By the end of the century their overseas trade had shrunk to negligible proportions, and many of them were glad to earn an illegal livelihood as middlemen in the internal trade. They thus joined the ranks of the despised wool-broggers, and became victims of the legislation they had promoted for their own selfish ends.

Acts and proclamations to control prices were meant to prevent the exploitation of the consumer—not necessarily the poorest consumer, since a good number regulated the price of wine, which was not the staple drink of the agrarian labourer. But corn and other victuals were regulated from time to time, as were also wood, wool and bowstaves, this last being of obvious concern to a nation that nominally still practised archery once a week. In addition the export of corn and fish was limited or forbidden in times of shortage; the year 1597, for example, finds the Privy Council carefully restricting the quantities of herring that may be exported from Yarmouth. All these attempts to control supplies and prices had little effect in the long run, however, and inflation continued with little abatement. The forces of demand and supply were more potent than those of the Tudor admini-

stration. But the price-rise might have been even more
catastrophic without government intervention, and at least
the periodic efforts of the crown did something to soften the
blow for those most vulnerable to bad harvests.

Controls on the export or import of certain goods were a
regular feature of Tudor legislation. Often these took the
form of a straightforward veto on the export of war materials.
Under this heading might be included also horses, whose
export was banned on at least nine occasions, starting in
1495. Bullion was also kept in the country as far as possible,
a policy that England pursued along with the Netherlands
and other states; the series of acts and proclamations on this
topic starts in 1489. This policy has seemed naïve and mistaken to some historians, but had some point to it when
trade balances had often to be settled in specie and mercenaries had to be paid in cash. Considerations of national
defence obviously played an important part here, while on
the other hand periodic vetos on the export of foodstuffs
showed a concern to relieve famine and keep food prices
reasonable. Other measures, however, had a more distinc-
tively economic character, and were intended to influence
the development of trade and industry. The attempt, so unpopular with the Merchant Adventurers, to limit the export
of unfinished woollen cloth below a certain price aimed to
provide work for the native cloth-finishing industry; the
obstacles were the resistance of the merchants and the back-
wardness of the industry itself in comparison with its rivals in
Germany and the Netherlands. Bans on certain imports,
such as that on foreign hats and caps in 1553, sought to protect the English manufacturer against competition—sometimes to revive the fortunes of a declining town, such as
Coventry.

These prohibitions did not add up to a comprehensive
system of protection for native industry, but they were
supplemented by patents of monopolies. These were much
more numerous, and by 1601 had multiplied to a point
where they constituted a major grievance. An angry house

of commons debated them at length, although the delicate question of the royal prerogative was involved. A member recited a formidable list of obnoxious patents that had been granted since the last parliament alone. The list included currants, iron, powder, cards, ashes, bottles, glasses, vinegar, sea-coal, steel, brushes, pots, salt, salt-petre, lead, oil and dried pilchards. Another indignant member expressed his surprise that bread was not on the list, and said that it would be before the next parliament if no steps were taken. Clearly the granting of monopolies had gone far beyond the protection of new or struggling industries, and had become a mere source of profit to such royal servants as had the sole right to manufacture or sell certain common consumer goods. It was alleged that prices had doubled or trebled, and that the public had been delivered into the hands of "bloodsuckers". The queen bowed before the storm, and revoked most of the monopolies that had come in for criticism. In the proclamation of November 1601, however, she insisted on her prerogative to issue such patents, and admitted significantly that many had been granted "to particular persons, which have sustained losses and hindrances by service at sea and land, or such as have been her Majesty's ancient domestical servitors, or for some other like considerations."One could hardly wish for a more frank admission that monopolies, in the government's own eyes, were a form of pension rather than a device for regulating the economy.

More consistent that measures to control industry—for whatever motive—were those intended to promote the growth of native shipping and seamanship. A series of acts, starting in 1485, insisted that Gascon wine and Toulouse woad be imported only in English ships under an English master and with a mainly English crew. This was not a new policy, since a more ambitious statute of Richard II had tried to insist that Englishmen should ship all goods in English bottoms. As with other acts, the effects were mitigated by the not infrequent issue of licences. A device tried by Cromwell in 1539 was to reduce the customs payable by aliens to the same level as that enjoyed by native merchants, a concession that was promptly followed by a proviso that it could be enjoyed only by aliens lading in English ships. This experiment ran for seven years, but was not renewed. A new approach was tried in 1563, when Wednesday was appointed as a day for eating fish (in addition to Friday), though licences to eat meat could be bought by individuals at a quite moderate tariff. The avowed aim of this measure was to increase the size of the fishing fleet and to encourage seamanship. How far such measures succeeded is uncertain. It was claimed in 1576 that the "political Lent" had brought about an increase of 140 fishing boats of between ten and thirty tons in the various ports of the east coast. Recent study suggests that these ports were already expanding their shipping before that date, with an especially rapid expansion in the 1540's. The increase up to 1550, however, was not as rapid in England as in the Netherlands, and moreover brought English shipping only up to about the same level as in the later 14th century. It was therefore an important and expanding industry, employing considerable capital and manpower, but its achievements must not be exaggerated— any more than the alleged stagnation of the preceding period. It might also be suggested that there were other causes for the expansion besides government encouragement. The rapid growth of the coal industry created a demand for more coastal shipping (the cloth trade demanded no great tonnage), and it is no surprise that Newcastle showed a particularly rapid and unbroken development—from 32 to 66 ships in the years 1500–1550. An expanding population would in any case need more fish to feed it, even without compulsory fish-eating on Wednesdays. The government's contribution may have been of only incidental importance.

The Tudor Poor Law has rightly attracted much attention from historians. Its successive stages show an increasingly humane and discriminating understanding of the problems of poor relief, and a recognition of society's duty to meet them. Sixteen statutes dealt with it specifically, reinforcing though not replacing the efforts of town corporations and private individuals. Its main provisions endured for good or ill down to the Poor Law Amendment Act of 1834. It offers perhaps the best evidence of Tudor paternalism in action, and the increased readiness of the state to intervene in social life.

The maintenance of law and order was no doubt a prime motive. Throughout the century we hear of the threat to peace presented by the sturdy rogues and vagabonds that infested the towns and swarmed over the countryside. They were sometimes discharged soldiers and sailors with no taste or aptitude for civil employment; the wars of the 1540's probably added to their numbers far more than did the dissolution of the monasteries. Sometimes they were mere scoundrels who preferred a life of idleness and were undeterred by the whippings prescribed by the law. With no regular police force to restrain them, such characters were a real menace and made the streets and highways unsafe to walk by day or night. On at least one occasion a well-known rogue intimidated by his threats of revenge the J.P. who had committed him; before the whole bench he "swore a great oath that if he were whipped it would be the dearest whipping to some that ever was" and he was eventually "delivered without any whipping or other harm, and the Justice glad he had so pacified his wrath." In 1585 there existed a flourishing school for London cutpurses at Billingsgate; enterprising lads practised the skill of extracting money silently from purses hung with bells, and earned for their proficiency the title of "public foister" or "judicial nipper". Less violent methods of parting the innocent from their money included games of cards and dice, the telling of fortunes and the reading of palms. The machinery of the law was inadequate to cope with all these malefactors, who even if apprehended could count on a good deal of popular sympathy. "In which default of justice many wicked thieves escape, for most commonly the simple countryman and woman, looking no farther than into the loss of their own goods, are of opinion that they would not procure a man's death for all the goods in the world." Something more was needed to deter and restrain the vagrant, and to provide prevention where cure was manifestly not to be had.

Not all vagrants were criminals, but even the most innocent beggar could be a burden upon the charity of his neighbours. Inevitably beggars congregated in the wealthier towns and parishes, who thus became burdened with numerous indigent "foreigners" in addition to their own poor. It was difficult to check on the credentials of every beggar, and charity could easily be abused. The citizens of Norwich were complaining in 1571 of beggars whose demands exceeded their real needs, and who spoiled and wasted the food given to them "very voluptuously". The desire of every parish to ease its total load, and to confine its almsgiving to deserving cases among its own inhabitants, was another motive towards reform.

Earlier Tudor statutes were almost purely punitive and deterrent, providing simply for the punishment of vagabonds and their removal to their place of birth or established residence. An Act of 1495 attempts no more than this. It was assumed that there was work for every able-bodied man in the kingdom and that the vagrant were unemployed by their own choice. This notion died hard, and to the end of the century writers tend to take for granted that rogues became such by choice rather than circumstance. Increasingly, however, a distinction was made between the deserving and undeserving poor, a distinction that first appears in 1531 between rogues who are to be punished and "aged, poor and impotent persons" who may solicit alms. Even more significant, perhaps, was the growing provision of machinery to enforce both the punitive and remedial legislation. Again the Act of 1531 set a precedent in making the J.P.'s responsible for enforcement, and five years later another important Act established the parish as the administrative unit for poor relief. It took longer to provide a system for raising adequate funds, since mere exhortations by curates of the parish (1536) or even by bishops (1550) did not prove sufficient. In 1563, therefore, compulsion was introduced, and J.P.'s were empowered to assess reasonable donations on the uncharitable and to enforce them on pain of imprisonment. In 1598 the financial problem was finally resolved by the institution of the poor rate, the basis of all future local taxation, with provision for poorer parishes to be subsidised by their wealthier neighbours. The administration of poor relief was to be in the hands of four overseers, appointed annually by the J.P.'s, who had power to levy the poor rate by distress and had responsibility for apprenticing poor children and maintaining houses for the impotent poor. Another Act of the same year provided for sturdy rogues to be whipped and sent to their own parish, and if deemed dangerous to be put in gaols or houses of correction. The final act of the series, that of 1601, did little more than repeat and codify the legislation of 1598.

By the end of the century, then, a fairly comprehensive system of poor relief had come into being. It is true that the law was still harsh towards the able-bodied unemployed, and that they were still held responsible for their own misfortune; the draconian legislation of 1547, however, allowing for branding and reduction to slavery, only lasted three years, and an act of 1576 had at least recognized the necessity of providing raw materials ("wool, hemp, flax, iron or other stuff") for them to work on. The impotent poor were maintained by the parish, and poor children apprenticed till the age of twenty-one or twenty-four. Adequate financial and administrative machinery for enforcement was provided. The passage of two centuries produced social changes that made the reforms of 1834 long over-due, but in 1601 England could boast of a more enlightened and efficient system of poor relief than any country in Europe.

The central government should not be given too much credit for this achievement, since local authorities acted well in advance of it. London instituted a compulsory poor rate as early as 1547, and converted the Bridewell for the maintenance of its poor five years later. Norwich took a census of its poor in 1570, and in 1571 set up elaborate machinery to deal with them, under the supervision of commissioners for the poor, deacons of wards and select women. Indiscriminate alms-giving was forbidden and charity put on an institutional basis, with separate provision for the different categories of the poor. It was claimed that the system both cleared the streets of beggars and benefited the city more than £3000, though a disquieting note is struck by the statement that the vagabonds are diminished to one-tenth of their former numbers "for the fear of the terror of the house of Bridwell. . . .". But grim as their institutions may have been, the citizens of Norwich had anticipated in 1571 the national system of 1598.

It can also be suggested that the national system was more impressive on paper than in actual performance. Careful study of parish accounts for Elizabeth's reign suggests that the statutory powers of local authorities were rarely invoked in practice, and that a poor rate was only levied in times of dire emergency. This continued to be true even after 1598, when these powers were increased. The available evidence suggests that only ten or eleven levies were made annually throughout England in the period 1560–1600, and that the total sum disbursed in poor relief was a little under £12,000. Levies were more common in rural parishes, which lacked the privately-endowed charities of the towns, but even here they were comparatively rare. W. K. Jordan estimates that in no year before 1660 was more than seven per cent of money devoted to poor relief raised by taxation. The poor rate was thoroughly unpopular, and in spite of objurgations and inquiries from the Privy Council was only raised as a last resort. It was private charity that bore almost the entire burden of poor relief down till 1660, and for a long time the great Elizabethan Poor Law operated only sporadically when famine and distress forced J.P.'s and parish officers to make use of it. As against the £12,000 raised by the parishes no less than £174,000 was given for poor relief by private donors in the same period, 1561–1600. The national system, comprehensive and progressive though it was, served only to supplement in emergency the work of private charitable enterprise.

A number of acts in the Tudor period related to particular towns and had only local significance. Some of these clearly had the defence of the realm in view. Special concern was shown in the reign of Henry VIII for the maintenance and restoration of various ports, Southampton, Plymouth and the western ports and havens all receiving statutory attention in the 1530's. A few such local acts were intended to curb the public nuisance caused by private individuals—men who erected weirs on navigable rivers like the Severn, for example. In both these directions Tudor governments acted for the national interest and the common good.

Other local acts were more dubiously in the public interest, though their preambles naturally alleged that this was the prime consideration. At least some of them can be shown to be the work of powerful pressure-groups that had achieved a temporary ascendancy. A case in point is the act of 1566 that gave the Shrewsbury Drapers a monopoly of the trade in Welsh cloth stapled in that town. This measure was doubtfully in the interests of the town, and it was not supported by the town council. Nor is it likely that concern for high standards in the cloth industry was the real motive—whatever the preamble to the act may have alleged. It seems in fact to have been due to a short-lived alliance between the drapers and shearmen of Shrewsbury that temporarily gained the ear of parliament. The shearmen's gain from the bargain was that traders in cloth were forbidden to engage in the finishing industry or to pay the shearmen in truck rather than money.

The act was repealed in 1572 as a result of a regrouping of alliances. The shearmen had now joined cause with the mercers, the drapers' principal rivals. In spite of heavy expenditure the drapers were unable to prevent the abolition of their monopoly, though the clauses of the 1566 act that protected the shearmen were retained. In the long run the drapers were to show greater staying-power than their rivals, but for the time being they had suffered a sharp set-back. In neither 1566 nor 1572 had the national or even the local interest of Shrewsbury been the real issue. Two egoistic groups had fought for their private advantage, making use of parliament for their own ends. Most local acts are not as well documented as this one, but it is unlikely that the Shrewsbury story was unique. In 1598 the queen forbade the further reading of two bills for the draining of fenlands, both of which had passed the two Houses and only required the commons' approval of amendments made by the lords. Sir John Neale is confident that the queen had good reasons for using her veto, but the reasons are not known. Is it not at least equally likely that some interested party had won the queen's or Cecil's ear and secured a timely intervention?

But the parliament of 1597–98 was certainly much more than an arena for sectional struggles. The commons were by now ready to take the initiative in economic and social problems, where previously it had lain with the crown. The main acts of 1597 were framed in committees of the house of commons. In the debates on tillage that arose from the urgent need to deal with the famine of that year some voices spoke indeed for economic individualism and for letting the forces of the market have free play. Others showed a more lively—if possibly ill-directed—concern for the poor, a stronger sense of social responsibility. "The eyes of the poor are upon this Parliament, and sad for the want they yet suffer. . . . We sit now in judgment over ourselves. . . . As this bill entered at first with a short prayer, 'God speed the plough', so I wish it may end with such success as the plough may speed the poor."

For the greater part of the 16th century, however, economic legislation had come mainly from the crown. Its meaning and intention have been variously interpreted. About the turn of this century writers like Schanz and Cunningham were stressing the continuity and consistency of government intervention in economic affairs. It was easy in retrospect to discern a pattern and system, and tempting to dignify this with the term "policy." It could be pointed out that Tudor governments steadily sought to divert a growing share of foreign trade into the ships and warehouses of their own subjects, and to oust foreign merchants from their privileged position on English soil. The so-called Navigation Acts, treaties such as the Magnus Intercursus of 1496, and the gradual contraction of Hansard privileges ending with closure of their Steelyard—all these could be adduced in evidence. The government could also be shown as a consistent enemy of agrarian enclosures, apart from one brief lapse during the rule of Northumberland in 1549–53. A sustained effort to enlarge and bolster up the gild system could be read into the great Statute of Apprentices (1563) and other enactments for particular crafts. The evolution of the Tudor poor law could be seen as a steady progress from mere harsh repression of vagrancy to enlightened care for the weak and helpless, culminating in the great act of 1601 that was to endure for more than two centuries as the basis of poor relief. It might be admitted that much of this legislation was conservative in character, but it could also be represented as evidence of far-sighted paternalism and the willingness of the central government to assume ever wider responsibilities for the material welfare of its subjects.

More recent writers have stressed the growing concern of the central government to obtain precise information as a preliminary to legislation—or even perhaps for its own sake. Cromwell's introduction of baptismal registers, the enclosure commissions of 1517 and 1549, the sheep census of 1549, the detailed memoranda on trade prepared for William Cecil— these can be seen as the beginnings of a more "statistical" approach to economic problems, even if the fiscal interests of the crown are also very much to the fore. The worth of some of these "statistics" is often very doubtful, but it can be and has been plausibly argued that the attempt to compile them at least shows forethought and deliberate planning. We are still a long way from the Welfare State, but its embryo can now be faintly seen.

An opposing school of thought, fathered by George

Unwin, holds that Tudor intervention in economic affairs was far from systematic or intelligently conceived. It was on the contrary random and arbitrary, both in principle and execution. It was not primarily the concern of any Tudor government to promote economic and social advance; the dominant concerns were always the maintenance of order, the waging of war, and the collection of money to make war possible. Agrarian enclosures and the spread of industry to the countryside produced social disorder and therefore had to be limited. Trade was a useful instrument of foreign policy, and merchants a useful source of revenue. When public order and war were not the paramount interests, then legislation was as often as not inspired by the selfish interests of some powerful pressure-group, some gild or trading company that had the ear of the government. It may be true that certain threads appear to run constantly through this legislation, but the supposed pattern and design are largely illusory, a construction of the historian writing with all the wisdom of hind-sight. Clearly the successive Tudor governments shared certain assumptions and prejudices, and these form a consistent element in their laws and proclamations; but that is not to say that they had an economic "policy" or that they knew where they were going.

It can likewise be suggested that much legislation, even when truly well-intentioned, was ineffective in practice because there was no machinery to enforce it. The good intentions of a Protector Somerset could be easily thwarted by the avarice of the enclosing landlord. The most vigorous minister could be blocked by the passivity or active obstruction of the local Justices of the Peace. With no widespread paid civil service or standing army the government simply could not impose its will. The administration of the law depended on the good pleasure of the country gentry, and they enforced only those parts of it that accorded with their interests and prejudices. They might co-operate to keep down wages, but not to pull down enclosures. The statute book is a record of pious hopes rather than real achievement.

Both these views have been stated in extreme forms, and clearly neither represents the whole truth. No modern historian would state the problem in so unqualified terms, though the balance of current opinion probably tilts towards the latter view, towards Unwin rather than Cunningham. To decide where, between the two extremes, the truth may lie we must look more carefully at the general issues raised.

A paramount aim of the Tudor government, like any government, was to keep order. In the absence of a police force or standing army prevention was much better than cure, since even a quite small disturbance might quickly reach alarming proportions. Revolts were expensive to put down at any time, especially if foreign mercenaries were hired for the job, as happened in 1549. For both political and financial reasons, therefore, the crown was anxious to forestall social unrest. At least a part of the government's concern over enclosures was inspired by the fear that agrarian discontent would provide a breeding-ground for other grievances—political, dynastic or religious—and that these might combine in a major revolt. Ket's rebellion in 1549 showed how quickly rebellion could grow out of economic and social grievances alone. On a much smaller scale the problem of vagrancy and unemployment could be serious in particular localities; in villages unprotected by a police force a few sturdy vagabonds could be a major threat to peace. In a more general way the Tudors feared that any social change might lead to disorder; hence the consistently conservative nature of legislation that sought to keep everyone in the station that he was born to and in the job he had been brought up to do. Here the gild and apprenticeship organisation supplied the natural machinery, and since by this time it had fallen into the hands of the merchants and employers, legislation to this end was inevitably class-legislation.

The government was also self-evidently concerned for the defence of the realm, a problem partly connected with that of the maintenance of order, since foreign princes might exploit unrest in England. The revolts of 1549 weakened England in her campaigns against France and Scotland. Agrarian unrest in vulnerable areas like the Isle of Wight was especially disturbing. The defences of the south coast in general were a constant concern, and a series of statutes throughout the century dealt specifically with the upkeep of harbours such as Southampton and Plymouth. Naval defence depended in part on the use of converted merchantmen, and the purpose of Tudor "navigation acts" was no doubt in part to increase England's war potential by stimulating both the building of ships and the training of sailors. Acts and proclamations forbidding the export of certain goods also had a military aspect. Clearly no government would gladly permit the export of munitions and horses in time of war. Bullion restrictions, too, were inspired by more than merely financial or economic motives. In an age when wars were largely fought by mercenaries, and mercenaries had to be paid in cash, a drain of specie meant a reduction in a country's capacity for war and a corresponding increase in the capacity of a possible enemy. There may also have been a conscious desire to make England more completely self-supporting in case of war, but on the whole it is more likely that bans on the export of grain arose from the immediate pressure of bad harvests than from a grand design to promote autarky. A wide-spread conviction that the export of raw materials merely gave work to foreign craftsmen, and produced in return a flow of idle fripperies, also played its part.

Fiscal considerations were also important. There is no room here for a full account of Tudor financial policy, nor even for much discussion of its impact on the economy and society. The Tudors suffered, like all contemporary rulers, from chronic shortage of money, mainly owing to rising prices, wars and rebellions, a more costly administration, and some courtly extravagance. Their main sources of revenue were the customs and direct taxes on land and movable goods, neither of which could be exploited to the full. The customs administration suffered from failure to take an adequate return from the cloth trade in the time of its greatest expansion—not till Mary's reign was a realistic rate imposed—and from failure to devise an efficient system of valuation that met the problems of inflation and merchant guile. It also suffered, no doubt, from smuggling and deliberate evasion, but these were probably less serious than failure to keep up to date with the Book of Rates, the official price-list by which goods were assessed in the customs house. When a merchant like Thomas Kitson in the 1530's could sell his goods at twice their customs valuation the government was clearly losing heavily. But perhaps it would not have paid in the long run to press the merchants too hard; the crown needed their co-operation in raising loans, and it would be folly to kill the goose that lent golden eggs. Similarly it was politically inexpedient to press the landed classes too much in trying to obtain realistic assessments of their wealth. Failure to do so meant that the yield from direct taxation fell at a time when prices were rising rapidly, and the difference could be made up only by demanding grants more often. But strict assessment would certainly have alienated the classes that the Tudors depended on for local government; even unpaid officials had their price. Just as Queen Elizabeth had to win at the peculations of her great officials, to whom she could not pay salaries commensurate with their services, so also she had to allow peers and gentry to escape with very easy tax payments. And since all classes resented direct taxation except for war purposes, the parliamentary subsidy was only a partial answer to the problems of inflation.

Two desperate remedies attempted to solve the dilemma did have considerable social and economic consequences. One was the sale of crown lands, which after 1540 included also the recently seized monastic estates. These sales enabled lawyers, merchants and gentry to buy new estates and round off old ones. They permanently weakened the financial power of the crown, but because most of the lands went at a fair price they did not create new wealth for their purchasers. The other desperate expedient was debasement of the coinage, practised from 1543–51. This brought temporary relief to a hard-pressed exchequer, but brought with it rapid inflation and the disruption of trade. The process was halted by Northumberland in 1551, but a fully restored coinage and the calling in of the debased coins had to await the efforts of Cecil and Elizabeth in 1560–61. This remedy was not tried again.

A fiscal element certainly entered into both the making of laws and their administration. The 1549 tax on sheep and cloth undoubtedly had as one of its objects to discourage the conversion of arable to pasture; the preamble to the act, however, represents it as a revenue-raising device, though this may have been intended to help it to pass a hostile house of commons. Projectors placing their ingenious plans before the government usually emphasised the increase in trade, and therefore in crown revenue, that would accrue from their schemes. The practice of granting licences to exempt individuals from statutes was also a financial asset. Licences could be issued, for example, to export wool elsewhere than to the Calais staple, to export undyed cloth of a higher value than that officially permitted, or to import wine and woad in foreign ships. Such relaxations were sometimes perfectly jus- tifiable, and the crown's exercise of this dispensing power quite reasonable. Under an able minister like Cromwell the power was not likely to be abused, and in the 1530's the num- ber of licences does not appear to have been excessive. But such licences could easily be used as a form of payment to officials and court servants, who could sell the licence to the merchants who would make use of it. This practice seems to have been quite common in Henry VIII's earlier years, when trading licences were often issued to gentlemen with no clear trading interests of their own. If this was done too frequently—though it is difficult to say if in fact this did happen—legislation might well be frustrated. In Eliza- beth's reign patents of monopoly likewise tended to become

6*

simply a perquisite, Walter Raleigh being one of the more notorious beneficiaries. Here again the system of government control was being used as a means to supplement inadequate salaries or simply to gratify favourites, and the ultimate cost was borne by the consumer, who paid a higher price for monopoly wares. A potential instrument of economic planning had become a mere fiscal device.

There was also a marked paternalistic note in much Tudor legislation, a real concern to do justice to all the crown's subjects and to maintain traditional moral standards. Enclosure laws were at least partly intended to alleviate hardship, and the development of the poor law shows increasing concern for the genuinely unfortunate, not only the permanent need to keep order. Price regulation was meant to maintain a system of "just" prices and keep essential foods within the means of the poor. That the government was successful in keeping wages rather than prices down does not prove a cynical disregard for the humble, but imperfect control over market forces. The crown further shared its subjects' intense suspicion of the middleman, one who made inordinate profits from minimal services. Repeated attacks were made on "engrossers", "forestallers" and "regraters", traders who either established brief monopolies in scarce goods or bought wares simply for a quick sale. Some of the criticism levelled at these notorious "takers of advantages" no doubt had a solid basis, but it is also clear that they were often made the scapegoats for economic distress that the government could not understand or remedy. The usurer was another target, the word meaning one who drove unfair bargains rather than simply one who charged interest on loans. Unpopular figure as he was, the crown could do little to curb his activities. Though the charging of interest was forbidden for most of the century it was impossible to block all the ingenious devices that money-lenders found to evade the law—an interest-charge was implicit in every bill of exchange, and loans could easily be made in over-valued goods that had to be paid for in cash. The "unfair bargain" was by its nature too ill-defined a term to lend itself to legislation, though the Court of Chancery did something to mitigate the harshness and inadequacy of the common law. But the Tudors and their ministers were not lacking in concern.

In addition to upholding traditional standards of decent and fair dealing, the government sought also to maintain standards of workmanship. This was clearly a major factor in apprenticeship legislation, though it might be argued that seven years was a long time to learn one of the simpler crafts, and that the system did also supply the employer with a good deal of cheap labour. The same concern emerges in the very frequent regulation of the cloth industry; here there was a real need to maintain the reputation of England's greatest export, though at the same time crown and parliament may have been over-impressed by the propaganda of the merchants, always ready to blame their inability to sell their cloths on the shoddiness of the manufacture. The regulation of other industries served to protect the English consumer against meretricious goods. It also, of course, maintained a large number of monopoly groups, and it is not altogether clear whether manufacturer or consumer benefited more from state intervention.

All these motives might well be mixed in a single legislative act, and it is difficult to say in any one case which predominated. Preambles to statutes may be misleading, since they sometimes state a pretext rather than a reason, or else emphasise only the reason most likely to appeal to a reluctant house of commons or populace. It is *a fortiori* harder still to say which of these themes predominated in Tudor economic legislation as a whole.

It cannot be assumed that all legislation originated with the crown or its ministers. Clearly no law would be passed if it directly conflicted with the will of Henry VIII or Elizabeth or ran counter to the plans of Thomas Cromwell or William Cecil. Their approval or neutrality was essential. Important bills would doubtless be scrutinised by the crown's ministers with some care. The royal **assent to bills that** had passed

both houses of Parliament was far from being a mere for-
mality. But this was a period when affairs of state took automatic precedence over the affairs of the "commonwealth",
and economic matters thus took second place to political
and religious ones: ministers primarily concerned with
effecting the breach with Rome or conducting a Scottish
war could direct only a small part of their attention and
energy to the affairs of gilds or trading companies. Cromwell and Cecil had an immense capacity for hard work, but
their time was limited and they had of necessity to lean on
the advice of experts. Because these are often shadowy
figures and their influence hard to assess, too much knowledge and wisdom may easily be attributed to their masters;
Cecil in particular has tended to be cited as the author of
every measure for which no other originator could be proved,
and the possible influence of Sir Thomas Smith or Sir
Nicholas Bacon ignored. Somerset's agrarian policy clearly
owed much to the informed advice of John Hales. Thus
while the crown and its ministers must bear final responsibility for legislation, this is not to say that the first idea
always sprang from the head of a minister. The often anonymous expert advisor played an important rôle.

The crown, moreover, did not lack advice from interested
parties outside the circle of its own officials. Towns might
plead for a reduction of their annual fee farm, or for the
establishment or maintenance of some lucrative staple. Gilds
and companies sought more effective monopolies to limit
competition; it is difficult to suppose that crown or parliament was as deeply concerned with the leather industry as the
numerous 16th century statutes regulating it might suggest,
and it is more likely that competing groups within it suc-
cessively caught the ear of ministers or members. Ingenious
private persons plied the government with schemes for the
betterment of trade and industry; usually these schemes
made provision for the inventor to enjoy some valuable right
of exploitation or inspection, whether for the dyeing of
native cloth, the organisation of marine insurance, or some

other activity. By the end of the century monopolies had multiplied to such a point that parliament protested, and a distinction was finally drawn between legitimate patents to protect new inventions and merely selfish monopolies of ordinary consumer goods.

Nor was legislation originating with the government always left unamended by parliament. It is now well known that the Elizabethan church settlement of 1559 was more radical than the queen intended, owing to the pressure of the reformers in the commons. Recent analysis of the Statute of Apprentices, once regarded as capital evidence of Cecil's far-seeing plans for the control of industry, has shown that it was likewise drastically modified in the course of its readings, and that the more significant apprenticeship clauses were among the additions. "Whatever it had which was new and forward-looking it owed to the house of commons." Lack of evidence makes it difficult to analyse many Tudor statutes in this way, but at least it is clear that the statute book cannot be used simply as an index of the crown's grand design for England's economy.

Parliament may also have had a negative influence that is impossible to estimate. It consisted mainly of landowners and employers, and clearly could not be expected to go far in legislating against its members' own economic interests. Too much should not be made of this, and it would be unjust to suggest that all legislation of this period was class-legislation. The landowners were prepared to pass acts against enclo-sures even during the "reactionary" régime of Northumber-land. But inevitably there were limits to their altruism, and a radical new deal for the poor was not to be expected. We often do not know the details of the bills that were re-jected; still less can we say how often a hopeful scheme never even reached the stage of being put into a bill because its rejection was anticipated. Probably this did not happen very frequently, since crown and landowner shared the same social assumptions and would not often come into conflict.

Execution of legislation was another question, as we have

seen in numerous instances. Responsibility lay with the
J.P.'s in most cases, voluntary officials who worked with the
assistance of the equally voluntary High Constables and
Petty Constables. The Commission of the Peace in every
county was made up of the more influential gentry, men of
the same calibre and interests as those who composed the
Tudor house of commons. Like them they could not be
pressed too far against their own interests. Overt opposition
to king or privy council was unlikely, but there was considerable scope for passive resistance. Just as the constables
—whose service was often very reluctant—had to be prodded
into action by the J.P.'s, so the J.P.'s in turn had constantly
to be set in motion by the council. Without such stimulus
offences against statutes and proclamations would go un-
prosecuted and unpunished. It was hard enough in any case
to conclude judicial proceedings in face of the apathy and
absenteeism of local juries, and obstruction by the officials
made effective action virtually impossible. Even if a new law
reached the statute book despite a reluctant house of commons, the J.P.'s could easily ensure that it remained a dead
letter merely by inaction.

The extent of this potential opposition must not be exaggerated, however. Membership of the bench was a prized
social asset, analogous to representing one's county in parliament. Exclusion from the Commission of the Peace would
mean serious loss of face in the intense competition for prestige that was such a feature of local life. Worse still, it would
probably mean the inclusion of a local rival. There were
practical considerations too. Justices regularly played a part
in tax-assessment and the selection of men for military service; it was as desirable to have one's own finger in this pie
as it was dangerous to leave such tasks to an unfriendly neighbour. Hence in spite of the onerous duties laid upon the
J.P.'s there was keen competition to get on to the bench. The
Chancellor was under constant pressure to enlarge the Commission of the Peace in every county, and the privy council
had to carry out periodic "purges" to reduce numbers and

remove undesirable individuals. Thus the central government had a very real threat at its disposal, and even passive opposition by the J.P.'s had to be kept within strict limits. Too much sloth meant loss of a valuable privilege.

Failure to enforce legislation strictly did not necessarily imply opposition or even sloth on the J.P.'s part. The Justices had to reconcile a number of local needs and interests, and social justice was not always best served by too thorough enforcement of the law. In periods of trade depression and unemployment the strict application of the apprenticeship laws could lead to unnecessary hardship, and at any time it was reasonable to allow exceptions for good workers long established in their trade. Thus for various reasons it is unfair to represent the Tudor J.P.'s as local oligarchs united in the defence of their own interests. The machinery of law-enforcement was certainly creaky, but conscientious Justices did exist, and the privy council was equipped if need be to deal with laggards. It is unlikely that England was worse administered than contemporary France, for all that the French king could boast of his army of paid civil servants, or that the amateurs in English local government were less amenable to central control than officials who had paid for their offices and could not be easily removed from them.

The imperfect machinery of officialdom was partly reinforced by individual enterprise. Tudor statutes often made provision for the private informer to share with the crown the fines arising out of any contravention of the new law. This saved the trouble of setting up special machinery for enforcement, and partly remedied the absence of a permanent police force. In like manner informers helped to make good the considerable deficiencies of the customs service. Informing was certainly a very active occupation in the 16th century, and probably more cases were brought before the courts by informers than by officials. The majority, perhaps, were initiated by individuals anxious to protect their own immediate interests—the gild members, for example, who resented the competition of rivals who had not served a regular apprenticeship. Some may have arisen quite simply from personal animosity or jealousy. A number of men, on the other hand, set up in business as professional informers, sometimes with a small network of agents to assist them. Whether either informer or government derived much benefit from this enterprise is open to grave doubt.

For the informer the pecuniary rewards were not very high. The fines actually imposed on offenders were often moderate, and the informer's half-share correspondingly low. A mere 10s. was often his reward for information under the apprenticeship or cloth acts. A very active professional informer, George Whelplay, apparently made only £22 out of three years' hard work in 1538–41. The costs of even a successful action might be considerable, and of an unsuccessful one still more, since the informer had to bear at least part of the successful defendant's costs. On the other hand some informers no doubt made money in unofficial ways. The mere threat of legal action might frighten some offenders into private composition with the informer, since even successful legal action was costly, especially in terms of working time lost. A poor offender might well find it cheaper to submit to blackmail than to face the costs of court action, since he would rarely recover his full costs. But it is unlikely that many informers made a large regular income from such shady transactions, and probably most had to make do with a very moderate return and an undesirable reputation.

The system was only doubtfully efficient from the government's point of view. It secured the services of unpaid prosecutors, but all the difficulties of securing conviction still remained. Juries were especially reluctant to find against a local man informed against by a "foreigner", and smuggling was already in the 16th century an almost respectable occupation. Blatantly guilty men could cheerfully go before a jury of their peers, and perjured juries were one of Star Chamber's most serious preoccupations. Moreover the unpopularity of the informers mounted in Elizabeth's reign, and legislation to restrict their activities—partly to clear the Westminster courts of trivial cases—was passed in 1576 and 1589. The system tended to bring the law into disrepute without making enforcement certain.

We should not, however, make too much of the government's difficulties. Whilst it is clearly inappropriate to talk of a "Tudor despotism", it would be equally exaggerated to suggest that the Tudors were quite unable to make their will effective. Direct opposition to the crown was rare, and the penalties of treason were heavy. The government could carry through revolutionary measures such as the break with Rome, the dissolution of the monasteries and the reformation in doctrine even when many of its subjects were hostile or unsympathetic. Those who challenged these steps shared the fate of More and Fisher, or the western rebels of 1549. But it was one thing to impose a single drastic measure, and quite another to ensure the steady maintenance of a host of regulations on religious, social and economic matters. The Tudor government was broadly successful in the former case, much less in the latter. Just as the recusancy laws of Elizabeths' reign were imperfectly enforced in the north and west, so we may doubt how far the cloth regulations or the apprenticeship laws were carried out in areas where the local authorities deemed them undesirable or inappropriate. Both the frequent re-enactment of existing legislation and the evidence of court records point to a wide gap between intention and fulfilment.

No very dogmatic conclusions can be drawn about Tudor economic "policy" or its success. Economic problems were always secondary for Tudor monarchs and their ministers, and economic measures often served non-economic ends. The paramount aims were peace and security. Prosperity was not an end in itself, nor could it be in so dangerous a century as the sixteenth. Nor can it be said that there was any master plan to guide the whole national economy. Certainly there were elements of consistency in the government's handling of economic problems, but if this consistency amounted to a policy it was still not an economic one. There was no fostering of the "middle classes" nor of "middle-class" values and ideas. Able men of relatively humble origins were indeed used in the administration. Merchants were praised when the government wanted their money. But the ways of the court were not those of the aldermen of London, and the successful civil servant or merchant made haste to set up as a great landowner. Social legislation was restrictive and conservative, aimed at maintaining the existing order. The value prized by the Tudors were those of the landowners, not those of the lawyers, merchants or manufacturers. But the government did show, in the midst of other preoccupations, an abiding concern for the needs of its poorer subjects. Its efforts to limit agrarian enclosures, to relieve famine, to provide for the destitute, all illustrate this. Even if its motives were mixed, even if concern for public order entered into all these cases, some desire for social justice cannot be denied. The growing frequency of government intervention at least argues a growing paternalism.

The exact degree of success achieved by the government is even harder to assess than its intentions. Where some success was attained we can never be sure how far it was due to government action rather than to other causes. Thus some success can be claimed for the government's encouragement of native shipping and for its poor law, though in both fields private enterprise probably achieved more than the state. Where legislation seems to have failed we cannot know that matters would not have been worse if no effort had been made at all. Enclosures may not have been seriously impeded by government action, but it is possible that without Wolsey's and Somerset's commissions they might have proceeded faster than they did. In heavy industry the very failure of the crown to enforce strict regulation was probably beneficial; mining and metallurgy flourished as they did not in France, where state control was more effective. The enforcement of economic legislation was always a problem, but the Tudors showed at least a growing concern to collect relevant information and to provide special machinery (as in the case of the poor law) where it was most necessary. It is difficult to see how they could have done much more than they did. No sixteenth century government had the knowledge, the means or even the wish to run a fully-planned national economy or set up a welfare state.

VI

CONCLUSION

THE ENGLAND THAT WILLIAM CAMDEN described in his *Britannia* in 1586 had not changed very much from the England of Leland's note-books fifty years before, and like his predecessor Camden was more interested in antiquity than in the contemporary scene. His observations on industry are a little perfunctory, though he found space to remark on the iron and glass manufactures of the Weald, which he described as resounding day and night with the water-driven hammers beating upon iron. In the north he noted the growth of Liverpool and Manchester, and estimated the population of Halifax (probably with some exaggeration) to number twelve thousand. Newcastle, where he ended his journeyings, he described as "the glory of all the towns in this country" and concluded his survey by quoting a doggerel verse in praise of coal:

> Why seek you fire in some exalted sphere?
> Earth's fruitful bosom will supply you here.

Unusually, for an Elizabethan, he rejoiced in the growth of London, "the epitome of all Britain, the seat of the British Empire". Much more typical was the resentful comment of the Customer for Sandwich in 1604:

> All our creeks seek to one river, all our rivers, run to one port, all our ports join to one town, all our towns make but one city, and all our cities and suburbs to one vast unwieldy and disorderly Babel of buildings, which the world calls London.

And Camden himself conceded that other towns had decayed as a result of London's increase.

If neither town nor country had undergone much change —apart from the depletion of forests and the growth of London—nor could it be said that the Tudors and their subjects had gone far in solving the economic and social problems with which the century began. Indeed many of these were aggravated in the 1590's by war, rebellion in Ireland, and harvest failure, so that the century ended on a sombre note. The prosperity of Elizabethan England was limited and precarious when the great queen died.

The period ended with a renewed outburst of depopulating enclosure in the midland counties, leading on to riots and bloodshed in 1607. It is remarkable that this should have happened at this particular date, since food prices were rocketing upwards and there was every apparent incentive to keep as much land as possible under the plough. Perhaps difficulties of transport prevented the midland farmers from exploiting the necessity of the Londoners and other townsfolk, though it hardly seems possible that this was the only explanation. At all events, the government was sufficiently alarmed to abandon its more permissive attitude towards enclosure, and to introduce new legislation against depopulation in 1597. Enclosure was still an obnoxious word at the end of the century, still linked in men's minds with the decay of husbandry and townships. John Norden, who well knew the economic advantages of enclosure for higher productivity, could describe depopulating enclosure as "the bane of a commonwealth, an apparent badge of Atheism and an argument of waspish ambition or wolvish emulation." It would be another half-century before such fears were greatly diminished.

There had, however, been some change of attitude. There were by this time more enclosures by agreement, and the enclosers were more often humble people. The word no longer meant only the ruthless aggression of a greedy landlord. There was wider recognition of the possible benefits of the process, and a greater flexibility in legislation. The act of 1597 allowed conversion of arable to pasture on an estate, provided that an equivalent area of grass were ploughed up. It was thus recognised that in some areas, at least, convertible husbandry called for the temporary replacement of tillage by grass. The early 17th century saw a widening of this recognition, and an act of 1608 allowed the enclosure of six Herefordshire parishes because "they do differ in the manner of their husbandry from many parts of the said county and other counties in the realm." Thus only five years after Elizabeth's death we have what Professor Beresford claims as the "first English pro-enclosure act".

The 1590's were not conducive to a stable and prosperous trade, and the apparent stability of the customs figures for cloth exports may well be misleading. New markets were only very partially exploited, and the development of the Russian and Far Eastern trades still lay in the future. There was still only one major export commodity, even though the New Draperies had been added to the broadcloths and kerseys that once dominated the Antwerp market. The disastrous failure of Alderman Cockayne's project in the reign of James I was to show, almost as drastically as the crisis of 1551, how dangerous it was for England to rely on a single product selling in only one area. That project was itself partly the result of growing criticism of the Merchant Adventurers, and this reminds us that they were still the most important single company in 1603, as in 1485. The Adventurers had more numerous and more vigorous rivals than they faced in the Calais Staplers, but again the rivalry was more apparent than real. The greater companies were all dominated by a narrow ring of wealthy Londoners, whose interests harmonised far more than they clashed, and the inclusion of aristocratic sleeping partners in the new joint-stock companies had not altered very much the structure of commerce. The real competition, not as yet very serious, was between the Londoners and the interlopers of the outports rather than among the Londoners themselves.

Imports still consisted mainly of luxury goods, and the same complaints of their superfluous nature were current. Fears of an adverse balance of trade and a consequent drain of specie abroad were as lively as ever. It is unfortunately not possible to say how far they were justified. But at least some voices were raised in defence of the import trade, however frivolous its content. Roger Bodenham, in a paper prepared for Burghley in 1571, had pointed out that foreigners could hardly buy our products if we did not buy theirs, and his memorandum shows in this respect an advance on the unrealistic views expressed in the *Discourse of the Common Weal*. On the other hand it could be said with some justice that foreign imports rarely contributed to native manufactures, and sometimes competed directly with them.

In the field of industry, too, there was in 1603 much more promise for the future than performance in the present. In spite of the growth of mining and metallurgy, in spite of the growing numbers of large-scale enterprises, it is fairly clear that Elizabethan England was not producing to capacity or using her resources of manpower to the full. Unemployment and vagrancy remained a problem throughout the century, and according to the verbal testimony of contemporaries (which cannot be checked by statistics) the problem was growing rather than diminishing. It seems reasonably certain that this unemployment was not merely seasonal or temporary, but a chronic condition. The country was not finding work to occupy an increasing population. In part this was no doubt due to failure to find satisfactory foreign markets. It was due also, and perhaps predominantly, to the high price of food in the towns, which reduced the domestic market for industrial goods. The towndweller of Elizabethan England had little money to spare when he had bought his daily bread. It might have been expected that the agricultural producer would profit from high prices enough to supply an alternative market, but farming technique was developing so slowly that this did not in fact happen. Neither farming nor industry was able to take advantage of its opportunities, and the relative failure of the one impeded the development of the other.

The monopolistic outlook of the gilds and companies, which tended always to assume that the market was strictly limited, probably contributed to underproduction and underemployment. Their restrictiveness was particularly unhelpful in a period of rising population. Where they remained powerful the tendency was towards increasing restriction and class-differentiation, though the London livery companies cannot be taken as typical of all. In provincial towns it was common for the trading oligarchy to organise the municipal government and economy to its own advantage. Happily the growth of new industries was escaping the control of gild and municipality in 1603, and Stuart industrial expansion could proceed at a faster rate.

The last decade of the century was also a critical period in the history of prices, which owing to war and crop-failure rose more rapidly in the 1590's than in any other period. This could not but mean acute hardship for the townsfolk, whose wages were held down by legislation enforced by the employing class. It also meant an acceleration of the social changes that were so unwelcome to the government. But while individuals climbed and descended the social ladder more rapidly than before, there had as yet been no major change in the social structure. The landed aristocracy, for all that its membership had somewhat changed since 1485, was far from ceding pride of place to its inferiors either in wealth or prestige. The Church had been stripped of much of its land, and the Crown had sold off much of its newly won possessions. The nobility had lost some of its military and political power, which now depended more on personal merit and less on the accident of birth. But the "gentry" had not, as a group, gained new riches, and they were only beginning to feel their political strength. The dominance of the "middle classes" was not yet established.

The government had also failed to solve a number of its

problems, and in 1601 had faced strong criticism for its indiscriminate issue of monopolies. It had not succeeded in containing industry within the confines of the towns and the gild system, and it had not even attempted to provide systematic protection for native manufactures. The customs system was purely fiscal in aim and character. Efforts to control prices were quite unavailing, though emergency measures against famine brought some relief and the currency reform of 1561 had partly remedied the damage caused by debasement. Most serious from the government's point of view was its failure to meet its own financial difficulties, which became acute in Elizabeth's last years. An "ordinary" revenue of £300,000 was enough for normal years, but few years were normal. The Irish rebellion alone cost nearly £2,000,000 in the years 1596–1601. Failure to revise either the level of custom or the Book of Rates after 1558 (the only major revision in the whole period) meant that the crown failed to increase its real income as prices rose. A similar failure to impose realistic assessments for subsidies meant that the propertied classes contributed much less than their fair share to the nation's expenses. It is true that subsidies were demanded and paid more frequently in the war years—they were granted by all the six parliaments of 1585–1601—but at the end of Elizabeth's reign the subsidy was still regarded as an exceptional measure; it had not, like the French Taille, become a regular source of revenue to be tapped annually at the government's discretion. Growing deficits were partly met by the sale of crown lands, of which some £876,000 were disposed of by Elizabeth. The crown's capital resources were in this way seriously diminished, and although income from crown lands may have risen by about one-third from 1558–1603 this increase did not keep pace with the rise in prices. Elizabeth left debts of only about £100,000, one-third of a year's revenue, but she had failed to maintain the financial strength precariously won by Henry VII. To have attempted this, however, might well have meant the forfeiture of political support from men of property. Elizabeth was not necessarily mistaken in preferring loyalty and willing service to money.

Against so many partial or total failures we can set a number of successes. English trade was more fully in the hands of its own merchants, and neither Italians nor Hansards took so large a share as in 1485 or even 1547. New markets had been found and would be developed in the coming century; it would be unreasonable to expect them to replace the old at a single stroke. The coal industry had seen a remarkable development, even if, as a contemporary alleged, the biggest profits went to the Dutch and French rather than to the native miners or merchants. Town life was more flourishing than it had been a hundred years before, even if its amenities were enjoyed by relatively few. No-one could deny the spectacular growth and wealth of London, though this was as often the subject of jealous complaint as of praise. Both public and private charity were better organised—if little greater in scale—to meet the problems caused by the failure of agriculture and industry to find food and work for a growing population. The poor in the towns were more numerous and (relatively) poorer than in 1485. But the foundations of economic expansion had been laid, and a better standard of living for all classes could be built upon them. Although the closing years of the Tudor age were harsh for most of the population, Elizabethan enterprise would eventually bring rich rewards.

SUGGESTIONS FOR FURTHER READING

Conyers Read's massive *Bibliography of British History: Tudor Period, 1485–1603* (1959) supplies a comprehensive and well classified guide to all books and articles on Tudor history published up to January 1957. It should be consulted by anyone requiring a detailed reading-list on any particular subject. Here it seems necessary to cite only a few of the standard works listed by Read, together with some of the more important books and articles that have appeared since January 1957.

Two brief general surveys are to be found in G. N. Clark, *The Wealth of England* (Oxford, 1946) and Sir John Clapham, *Concise Economic History of Britain* (Cambridge, 1949), though both require some revision in the light of recent research. There is also much useful material in A. L. Rowse, *The England of Elizabeth* (London, 1950), though the author tends to fix his gaze on the upper levels of society. Much the most useful collection of contemporary documents is R. H. Tawney and Eileen Power, *Tudor Economic Documents* (3 vols., London, 1925).

A very helpful short survey of the enclosure problem is provided by Joan Thirsk, *Tudor Enclosures* (Historical Association Pamphlet, 1959). The classic study of the question is R. H. Tawney, *The Agrarian Problem in the Sixteenth Century* (London, 1912). A more recent study, from a different approach, is the important work of M. W. Beresford, *The Lost Villages of England* (London, 1954). E. Kerridge, "The movement of rents, 1540–1640" (Economic History Review, 1953) is an important contribution to the discussion. Other works that should be consulted on Tudor agrarian history include W. G. Hoskins, *Essays in Leicestershire History* (Liverpool, 1950) and Joan Thirsk, *English Peasant Farming. The Agrarian History of Lincolnshire from Tudor Times* (London, 1957). S. T. Bindoff, *Ket's Rebellion, 1549* (Historical Association Pamphlet, 1949) is an admirable short summary of the main agrarian rising of the period.

There is as yet no major study in English on the Merchant Adventurers in the 16th century. Their early development and organisation are covered by two chapters in E. Carus-Wilson,

Medieval Merchant Venturers (London, 1954) and some part of their later activities by G. Unwin. "The Merchants Adventurers' Company in the Reign of Elizabeth" in *Studies in Economic History* (London, 1927). The history of the Staplers is briefly traced in the introduction to E. E. Rich (ed.), *The Ordinance Book of the Merchants of the Staple* (Cambridge, 1937). The Spanish trade in the early Tudor period is dealt with by G. Connell-Smith, *Forerunners of Drake* (London, 1954), and the declining fortunes of Tudor Southampton by A. A. Ruddock, *Italian Merchants and Shipping in Southampton, 1270–1600*. Changes in the character of English trade following the crisis of 1551 are discussed by F. J. Fisher, "Economic trends and policy in the sixteenth century" (Economic History Review, 1940). For the Elizabethan period there are the scholarly works of T. S. Willan: *The Muscovy Merchants of 1555* (Manchester, 1953). *The Early History of the Russia Company*, 1553–1603 (Manchester, 1956) and *Studies in Elizabethan Foreign Trade* (Manchester, 1959)—the last being valuable for its essays on the activities of interlopers and the provincial ports, and for its detailed survey of the trade with Morocco. Finally, there are some helpful essays in G. D. Ramsay, *English Overseas Trade during the Centuries of Emergence* (London, 1957), and some valuable information in the same author's edition of *John Isham's Accounts, 1558–1572* (Northamptonshire Record Society, Vol. xxi, 1962).

For the woollen industry the standard work is again by G. D. Ramsay, *The Wiltshire Woollen Industry in the Sixteenth and Seventeenth Centuries* (London, 1943), though the older works of H. Heaton, *The Yorkshire Woollen and Worsted Industries* (Oxford, 1920) and E. Lipson, *English Woollen and Worsted Industries* (London, 1921; rev. ed. 1953) may still be used. An interesting recent article on rural industry is by Joan Thirsk, "Industries in the Countryside" in *Essays in the Economic and Social History of Tudor and Stuart England,* ed. F. J. Fisher (Cambridge, 1961). On the coal industry the indispensable work is J. U. Nef, *The Rise of the British Coal Industry* (2 vols., London, 1932); the same author provides a more general survey in "The progress of technology and the growth of large scale industry in Great Britain, 1540–1640" (Economic History Review, 1934), and a useful comparative study in *Industry and Government in France and England, 1540–1640* (American Philosophical Society, 1940). For the Midland iron industry, W. H. B. Court, *The Rise of the Midland Industries, 1600–1838* (London, 1938) has some helpful introductory chapters. For gild organisation there are G. Unwin, *Industrial Organization in the Sixteenth and Seventeenth Centuries* (Oxford, 1904) and *The Gilds and Companies of London* (London, 1908).

Three studies of provincial towns are W. T. MacCaffrey, *Exeter, 1540–1640* (Harvard, 1958); J. W. F. Hill, *Tudor and Stuart Lincoln* (Cambridge, 1956) and W. G. Hoskins, "An Elizabethan provincial town: Leicester" in *Studies in Social History*, ed. J. H. Plumb (London, 1955).

The "cost-of-living index" compiled by E. H. P. Brown and S. V. Hopkins is printed in Economica, 1956. A very important recent article on the subject is that by Y. S. Brenner, "The inflation of prices in early sixteenth century England" (Economic History Review, 1961). The impact of the inflation on the aristocracy and gentry has been the subject of a heated controversy between R. H. Tawney, L. Stone, H. R. Trevor-Roper and J. P. Cooper; a convenient summing-up and judgment is supplied by J. H. Hexter in "Storm over the Gentry", reprinted in *Reappraisals in History* (Aberdeen, 1961). In the same volume appears "The myth of the middle class in Tudor History"—which effectively disposes of the myth. Two valuable social studies are M. Campbell, *The English Yeoman in the Tudor and early Stuart Age* (Yale, 1942) and M. E. Finch, *The Wealth of Five Northamptonshire Families, 1540–1640* (Northants. Record Society, Vol. xix, 1956). R. H. Tawney, *Religion and the Rise of Capitalism* (London, 1926) remains a classic work in the face of much controversy. For the charitable activities of Tudor merchants and others the indispensable works are those of W. K. Jordan, *Philanthropy in England, 1480–1660*; *The Charities of London, 1480–1660* and *The Charities of Rural England, 1480–1660* (London, 1959, 1960, 1961).

Government economic activity has received comparatively little detailed attention, apart from the Statute of Artificers which has been examined by R. K. Kelsall, *Wage Regulation under the Statute of Artificers* (London, 1938); M. G. Davies, *The Enforcement of English Apprenticeship, 1563–1642* (Harvard, 1956); and S. T. Bindoff (who examines the drafting of the act) in *Elizabethan Government and Society: Essays presented to Sir John Neale*, ed. S. T. Bindoff (London, 1961). Both Tawney and Beresford do, however, deal with agrarian policy in their works on the enclosure movement. E. M. Leonard, *The Early History of English Poor Relief* (Cambridge, 1900) is still a standard work, though weak on the subject of enforcement; it should be supplemented by G. R. Elton, "An early Tudor Poor Law" (Economic History Review, 1953). G. R. Elton, "Informing for profit" in *Star Chamber Stories* (London, 1958) gives an instructive case history of the practical difficulties of enforcement. F. C. Dietz, *English Government Finance, 1485–1558* (Univ. of Illinois, 1920) and *English Public Finance, 1558–1642* (New York, 1932) are still indispensable, though the figures should be treated with caution. Government failure to raise an adequate revenue, and the reasons for this failure, are demonstrated by J. Hurstfield, *The Queen's Wards* (London, 1958) and H. Miller, "Subsidy assessments of the peerage in the sixteenth century" (Bulletin of the Institute of Historical Research, 1955). Failure to exploit the customs system to raise revenue or direct trade is shown by T. S. Willan, *A Tudor Book of Rates* (Manchester, 1962).

P. J. Bowden, *The Wool Trade in Tudor and Stuart England* (London, 1962) appeared too late to be effectively used in the present work; it contains much valuable information both for agrarian and industrial history.

INDEX